Following Jesus
First Steps on the Way

Harold Percy

Anglican Book Centre
Toronto, Canada

1993
Anglican Book Centre
600 Jarvis Street
Toronto, Ontario
Canada M4Y 2J6

Typesetting by Jay Tee Graphics Ltd.

Canadian Cataloguing in Publication Data

Percy, Harold
   Following Jesus

ISBN 0-921846-55-X

1. Christian life – 1960–　. I. Title.

BV4501.2.P47 1993　　　248.4　　　C93-094015-6

Table of Contents

To Kathy, my life companion,
and to Joel,
Benjamin,
Rachel,
and Robbie,
who, I pray,
will grow up to be faithful followers of Jesus

Preface

For the past several years at Trinity Anglican Church, Streetsville, I have been leading a six-week course entitled "Following Jesus: First Steps." This course is designed for those who have recently made or renewed a decision to live as followers of Jesus, and for those who feel that they would benefit from a refresher course on the basics of faith development and spiritual growth. The stated purpose of the course is "to help you grow in your ability to live out your decision to be a follower of Jesus with a sense of confidence, joy, and expectation." This book represents much of the content of that course.

Over the course of many years' experience as a parish priest in the Anglican church I have observed that many people who participate regularly and willingly in the life of the church do not have a sense that they are making progress in the areas of faith development and spiritual growth. This absence is often accompanied by a lack of confidence in their understanding of the Christian faith and their ability to live it faithfully and consistently. The result is that there is often fear, anxiety, and frustration, where there could be joy, excitement, and enthusiasm.

This book is written for such people in churches all across the country and for their clergy who would love to help them, but who, for various reasons, find it difficult to do so. This book can be read individually by small groups which meet for Christian learning and growth or as the basis of a course which is part of a parish's adult faith development program. It emphasizes basic biblical information important to growing Christians and presents practical "next steps" to faith development and spiritual growth.

I would like to express my gratitude and appreciation to all the parishioners of Trinity Anglican Church, Streetsville, who have participated in our Following Jesus and Christian Basics courses over the past four years. Your enthusiastic participation, your questions, your comments, and your insights have been a source of constant encouragement and inspiration to me. Most of all, I would like to thank Diane Toycen, my colleague in ministry at Trinity, who has been involved from the very beginning in the preparation, refinement, and presentation of these courses, and to whom I owe more than I can ever express or repay.

Introduction

At the very heart of the Christian faith and life stands the invitation of Jesus to "come and follow me." There are many possible responses to this invitation but the only one that actually starts us on the journey is yes. Spoken in response to the invitation of Jesus to follow him, the single word *yes* is the most eloquent and powerful prayer in all the world.

This book is for people who have heard this invitation to follow Jesus and have said yes. Whether this is a decision you have made recently, or one that you made long ago and perhaps recently affirmed, this book is intended to help you to live out this life-changing decision with a sense of confidence, joy, and expectation.

A New Life in a New Family

The Bible uses many images from everyday life to describe what happens when someone turns to Jesus and begins to follow him. One of these is the image of starting a new life. Turning to Jesus and beginning intentionally to live as one of his followers is just like being born again. But this time we are born into the family of God. In the first chapter of John's gospel it is described like this:

> To all who received him (Jesus), who believed in his name, he gave the power to become children of God who were born, not of blood or the will of the flesh, or of the will of man, but of God. (John 1:12)

Growth Is Important

Being born is a significant event. But it is only a beginning. We all celebrate the birth of a baby with great joy, but our joy goes far beyond the simple fact of birth. It involves the anticipation that the new-born child will begin to grow and develop. If this baby does not grow normally, there is great concern: joy quickly turns to sorrow.

Similarly, when we are born into God's family there is the expectation that we will grow. We start out as babes in the faith and grow towards spiritual maturity. This involves learning how to follow Jesus faithfully and consistently. It involves an ever-expanding awareness of what God is doing in us and around us, and knowing how we can play a significant part in the work that God is doing. It involves, throughout the course of our lives, growing more and more to be like Jesus.

Food and Exercise

In order to experience healthy physical growth we need many things. Two of these essentials are food and exercise. These are needed not only in infancy, but throughout the whole of life. As followers of Jesus we need spiritual food and spiritual exercise in order to experience and sustain healthy spiritual growth and become mature Christians.

The food we need to nourish us in our spiritual growth is scripture, worship, and community. Our exercise will be prayer, ministry, and stewardship. If we have only food, our growth will not be healthy; if we have only exercise we will not last. Both food and exercise are required for healthy growth.

FOOD	EXERCISE
Scripture	Prayer
Community	Ministry
Worship	Stewardship

All of these elements must be kept in balance. Sometimes Christians become so enthusiastic about reading the scriptures that they neglect worship or responsible membership in the community of God's people. Their heads are filled with biblical knowledge, but they haven't found any meaningful way to put into practice what they have learned. Their Christian faith soon becomes dry and arid.

Others become so enthusiastic about some area of ministry that they enjoy, that they neglect the scriptures and worship. They are soon in danger of wandering down blind alleys, rather than following where Jesus is leading. Others become so enchanted with the idea of a loving community that they eventually lose sight of the standards to which the scriptures call followers of Jesus.

Careful, balanced attention to each of these elements will result in healthy, balanced spiritual development. In the following chapters we will consider each element in turn.

God is inviting you to become more than you have ever imgined you could be. Following Jesus, growing to be like him, and sharing in God's work is an adventure that lasts a lifetime. Let's get growing!

FOOD	EXERCISE
Scripture	Prayer
Community	Ministry
Worship	Stewardship

Scripture

Our Guide on the Journey

Holiday sections in newspapers and magazines frequently feature articles offering tips for travellers. Travel writers offer advice on what to wear in Europe in the springtime, or how to make a three-day journey by car with your children and live to tell the tale. There are suggestions of things to do and see that will add pleasure to the journey, and warnings of what should be avoided at all costs.

As we set out on our exciting adventure of learning to live as followers of Jesus, the Bible will be our indispensable companion and guide. As we seek to grow towards Christian maturity, scripture will be a staple of our spiritual diet. The Bible will also provide light for our pathway and protection from danger as we follow in the steps of Jesus.

Food for the Journey

Setting out on a journey of any length, all travellers know that they must plan to eat or the trip will quickly turn into a disaster. For some, finding nice restaurants and enjoying fine dining constitutes one of the highlights of the trip. Others eat more simply, frequenting the fast food outlets along the way. Still others pack as much food as they can, preferring to prepare their own meals.

The Bible has some advice in this regard for pilgrims on their journey through life. The Old Testament book of Deuteronomy tells us that one does ''not live by bread alone but by every word that comes from the mouth of the Lord'' (Deuteronomy 8:3).

The Bible reminds us that our deepest yearnings can never be met by the mere satisfaction of physical appetites. The ultimate reality that we seek is spiritual.

In this age of consumerism it is easy to lose sight of this essential fact. We are assaulted relentlessly by skilfully produced, high-powered enticements telling us that satisfaction and fulfilment will be ours with our next acquisition. But our appetites are insatiable. We always seem to need more. Enough is always just a little more than we have at present. It seems that most people are trying to accomplish the incredible feat of living on 110 per cent of their income. Far from leading to satisfaction, this is a sure-fire recipe for stress and anxiety.

Years ago, seated beside a well in the heat of the noonday sun, Jesus spoke to a woman who had been severely abused by life. Motioning to the well from which she had come to draw water, he said to her:

> Everyone who drinks of this water will be thirsty again, but those who drink of the water that I will give them will never be thirsty. (John 4:13–14)

In the scriptures we discover the word of God revealed in Jesus. This word is food and drink for the soul, refreshing those who have grown weary in the grinding pursuit of the shallow values of this age and in the service of its false gods.

Light for the Path

Walking in the darkness can be a frightening (to say nothing of dangerous) experience. Even if the darkness doesn't completely blind us, it can certainly distort our perception. We can be completely oblivious to lurking danger while objects that are absolutely harmless take on menacing forms.

It is possible to go through life walking in spiritual darkness. It is easy to forget that we are spiritual beings, created to live in friendship with God. In other words we lose our way. We can walk into walls, fall into ditches, trip over boulders, venture down dead-end pathways. We can be oblivious to very real dangers while fearing the harmless and the helpful.

However the scriptures shine light on the pathway and help us to travel with confidence and joy. By speaking the truth to us about God and ourselves they throw light on the pathway. As a poet wrote centuries ago in one of the psalms of Israel: "Your word is a lamp to my feet and a light for my path" (Psalm 119:105).

Protection for the Traveller

Travelling can be dangerous. Particularly during summer holiday weekends our newspapers carry tragic stories of the carnage on our highways. In the ancient world the traveller faced potential danger at every turn. Our journey as followers of Jesus is a hazardous journey as well, often leading through hostile territory. Christians understand that life is lived in the context of spiritual warfare.

Much of the Bible is simply unintelligible without the assumption of the reality of evil. In the service of Holy Baptism in *The Book of Alternative Services* of the Anglican Church of Canada, candidates for baptism are asked the following questions:

> Do you renounce Satan and all the spiritual forces of wickedness that rebel against God?
> Do you renounce the evil powers of this world which corrupt and destroy the creatures of God?
> Do you renounce all sinful desires that draw you from the love of God?

These questions put the matter of spiritual warfare clearly into perspective. Those who choose to live as followers of Jesus understand that there are evil powers working in opposition to God thwarting God's purposes. When we make the decision to live intentionally as followers of Jesus, as the service of baptism makes clear, we find that we are involved in the battle against evil.

There is no unanimous agreement amongst Christians on the exact nature of these evil powers. Opinions vary from very liberal to very conservative. Some believe that such a portrayal of evil is to be understood in a metaphorical sense, while others take it quite literally. Those with differing opinions on this matter have no need to quarrel with one another about it. It is enough to agree that there is opposition to God's purposes and that this opposition results in hideous and tragic destruction of what could be truly beautiful and good.

To be effective in dealing with an enemy we must know three things. We must know the enemy's objective, weapons, and tactics. In the Bible we learn that the purpose of these evil powers is to destroy God's creation and to frustrate God's purposes. For this enemy, the aim is simple chaos. To have people wandering in darkness and without direction is victory.

The enemy's favourite weapon is the simple lie, and the favourite tactic is quite unsophisticated deceit. This enemy deceives us into believing simple lies about ourselves and about life that will leave us lost and wandering. Experience tells us about how easy it is to live as if the point of life is to get ahead, or to be successful, or popular, or powerful. These lies are simple but seductive.

In the Bible the schemes and distortions of the evil powers are exposed, and God's truth, revealed in Jesus, enables us to see through the lies of the evil powers which seek to lure us from the love of God. It is interesting to note that Jesus rebuffed every attempt the devil made to deflect him from his purpose by quoting from the scriptures. The truth of God is the best protection there is from the lies of evil.

Reading the Bible: A Mystery

Let's face it. For most of us the Bible is a mystery. All things considered, we might be forgiven for being less than enthusiastic about the suggestion that Bible reading is absolutely essential to the diet of healthy, growing Christians.

Perhaps, like many others, you have made a valiant and determined effort to read the Bible but have given up, more frustrated than enlightened. One or two such experiences quickly lead to the conclusion that this book is best left to the professionals. Most of us have better things to do than frustrate ourselves by attempting the impossible. Your confusion and frustration are perfectly understandable. After all, the Bible is not just one more book like all those other books with which we are familiar and comfortable.

First of all, it was written a long time ago in ancient languages which most of us have no hope of or interest in ever learning to read. It was written in cultures vastly different from our own, by people and to people whose thought patterns, values, and understanding of the world were quite different from ours.

Adding to the confusion, unlike most books with which are familiar, the Bible does not read in a straight line from the beginning to the end. Nor is its subject matter neatly arranged in carefully sequenced chapters. (For example, if we want to learn about prayer, we cannot simply turn to the index of our family Bible and look up the page number for the chapter on prayer.)

To read the Bible with understanding, enjoyment, and pleasure we must be able to approach it without feeling overwhelmed or intimidated. A bit of background information should help to remove some of the mystery and enable us to pick up the Bible with a little more confidence.

Removing the Mystery

One Book/Many Books

Take your Bible in your hand. Simply look at it, feel its weight, fan through its pages. The first thing you need to know is that this is not a single book; it is a collection of books, written at different times, by different people, for many different reasons. In fact, it is more appropriate to think of the Bible as a library than as a single book. This explains why it is often frustrating to try to read the Bible in a straight line, from first page to last. We don't usually enter a library and simply choose the first book inside the door, and then continue reading through every book until we have reached the back of the room. We are much more selective than that. A library contains many different kinds of books. So does the Bible.

The Bible contains sixty-six different books, written over a long period of time — more than one thousand years. In addition, much of the material in these books had a long period of oral transmission before it was ever written down, and comes from a number of different cultural and historical situations. These sixty-six books were written by at least forty different authors, in addition to various editors who had a hand in giving them their final form. As in any library, these books represent many different types of literature, including history, poetry, stories of all kinds (fiction and non-fiction), biography, political documents, legal codes, and correspondence.

In thinking of the Bible as a library, think of a library that has two floors. These two floors correspond to the two major divisions of the Bible, the Old Testament and the New Testament. There are thirty-nine books in the Old Testament and twenty-seven books in the New Testament.

The dividing line between these two floors is the birth of Jesus. All of the books in the Old Testament were written before the birth of Jesus. Christians believe that these books, while dealing with the historical realities of the situations in which they were written, also anticipate the life and ministry of Jesus. The books in the New Testament were written after the birth of Jesus, and interpret his life, death, and resurrection.

The Story They Tell

The Old Testament begins with the story of creation, and goes on to relate the history of the people of Israel, beginning with the story of God's promise to Abraham that his descendants would grow into a great nation through whom the whole world would be blessed. This history is told with all its twisting and turning, its peaks and its valleys, its splendour and its horror.

Written in the Hebrew language, it features dramatic stories of political intrigue, horrendous stories of war and violence, and remarkable stories of individual heroism, nobility, and weakness. It is important to note that this history is always interpreted in terms of Israel's unique status as the people of God.

The New Testament was written in Greek. It tells the story of Jesus and describes the beginnings and early growth of the church. Its central focus is the resurrection of Jesus, following his crucifixion by hostile authorities.

In the New Testament we read the narratives of the life of Jesus, including some of his teaching and the stories he told, along with magnetic accounts of some of his personal encounters with a wide variety of people in many different circumstances. We also read of Jesus' closest followers as they puzzled and tried to make sense out of what was happening to them.

We read of Paul, his remarkable conversion and subsequent career travelling throughout the Mediterranean world, speaking about Jesus to all who would listen. Those who believed in Jesus formed small churches in various cities, and we read of some of their struggles as they slowly grew towards Christian maturity.

A Bigger Story

But throughout the pages of the Old and New Testaments a

much bigger story unfolds. This is the story of God's overwhelming love for us, and God's unending concern for our well-being. In this story we learn of God's purposes in creation. As the unique status of the human family within this creation is revealed, we discover that we have been invited into a special relationship with God and entrusted with the awesome responsibility of caring for all of God's creation.

This bigger story tells of our rebellion against our place in creation, and our insistence on claiming our independence from God. It tells of God's relentless, loving pursuit of us, calling us back in order to save us from ourselves and rescue us from the destructive forces of evil. It tells of the gracious invitation we are offered to come home and to enjoy the life with God for which we were created.

A major focus in this story is the formation of a special community of people known as the people of God. This community consists of those who respond to God's invitation, and who set out to live a new kind of life in friendship with God. This community lives as a witness to the existence and character of God, calling a lost world to return to the source of its life and meaning. As those who are learning to live as followers of Jesus, we learn from the Bible that we are a part of this special community in our own day.

A Word from Beyond

It will come as no surprise that among Christians there are many different opinions as to how the Bible is to be interpreted. Theological libraries are filled with countless learned volumes (ancient and modern) written by brilliant theologians on the subject of biblical interpretation. Needless to say, there is no unanimous agreement among them as to what it means to say the Bible is God's word to us, or what is meant by the theological concepts of biblical inspiration and revelation.

This should come as a relief to us. If the best minds of the church have not been able to agree on such complex matters, surely it is not up to you or to me to solve the riddle and pronounce the final word. It is enough to say that in every age, Christians have regarded the Bible as the book above all books. In fact, the very name *Bible* simply means *book*. The Bible is *The Book.*

Christians believe that the Bible is much more than an interesting book in which various thinkers have shared with us their thoughts about God. On the contrary, in this book we discover God's thoughts about us. Through many different writers, over a long period of time, God shares with us the story of why we were created and what our life is about. We learn of God, and where we fit into God's eternal purposes. In the Bible we discover how to live life as God intends it to be lived, in order that we might experience life in all its fullness.

To put it quite simply, Christians believe that the Bible is God's word to us from beyond. We believe that in some miraculous way the Bible speaks to us about life from God's point of view, rather than ours.

Getting Started

Coming to the Bible as one who has recently made or renewed a decision to live intentionally as a follower of Jesus, begin with the New Testament. Remembering our comparison with the library, this means that we are going directly to the second floor. The books on the first floor look interesting and we hate to pass them by, but there will be plenty of time for them later. First things first.

In the New Testament we find two main categories of books, gospels and epistles. In addition to the gospels and epistles there is a book called the Acts of the Apostles which describes the early development of the church, and at the end of the New Testament the Book of the Revelation. This latter is a fascinating book, but is certainly not the place for a relative newcomer to Bible reading to begin!

The Gospels

The first four books of the New Testament are called gospels.
The word *gospel* comes from an old Anglo-Saxon word which
means good news. The gospels are books which tell the good
news about Jesus. Look at the first verse of the gospel of Mark:
''The beginning of the good news of Jesus Christ, the Son of
God.'' The author is essentially saying, I am writing this book
in order to tell you the good news about Jesus.

When reading the gospels it will be helpful to know that
while they contain many details of Jesus' life, they are not really
biographies of Jesus. For one thing, they leave out too much.
We learn virtually nothing of Jesus' childhood, his home or
family life, his education, or the people who may have had
a significant influence on his life and thinking. There is little
hint of any of the experiences or influences that shaped his
spiritual development. There are no interviews with childhood
friends or relatives.

Nor is the material that is included in the gospels evenly
weighted, as one might expect from a carefully composed biography. For example, approximately forty per cent of the material in John's gospel deals with the last week of Jesus' life.

The writers of the gospels were not interested in portraying
a typical day or week in the life of Jesus either. As we read
the different gospels it becomes clear that much of the material is arranged topically rather than sequentially. The writers
seem to be more interested in topics and themes than in the
sequence in which events took place, hour by hour and day
by day.

On the other hand, the gospels are more than memories
and random collections of various statements attributed to Jesus
or anecdotes about him. These authors were not writing simply to help keep the memory of Jesus alive. The writers of the
gospels had a noble and lofty purpose which was nothing less
than to tell the story (the good news) of God's saving activity
in the life, ministry, death, and resurrection of Jesus of

Nazareth. They had come to believe that Jesus was the Son of God and the fulfilment of God's redeeming activity in the world as promised in the Hebrew scriptures. They wanted to share this news with the world.

The story begins with the birth of Jesus in Bethlehem, as told by Matthew and Luke. Mark and John do not mention Jesus' birth. The only passage in any of the gospels that even mentions Jesus' childhood is Luke 2:41–52.

The gospels begin the account of Jesus' public ministry with the story of his baptism by John the Baptist. The period of his public ministry was about two or three years at the very most. This ministry began in Jesus' native province of Galilee in the north, (his home town was Nazareth), and culminated in his arrival in Jerusalem at Passover time.

The centrepiece of this story is the crucifixion of Jesus by hostile authorities, followed by his resurrection from the dead three days later. The gospel writers want us to know that the resurrection is the very heart of the good news.

The purpose of these writers is not only to report but also to convince. They want to persuade their readers of the truth of the events they narrate and to lead them to faith in Jesus. The author of John's gospel makes this very clear:

> Jesus did many other miraculous signs in the presence of his disciples, which are not recorded in this book. But these are written that you may believe that Jesus is the Christ, the Son of God, and that by believing you may have life in his name. (John 20:30–31)

Where Did the Gospels Come from?

Although they are placed at the beginning of the New Testament, the gospels were among the last New Testament books written.

As the apostles and their earliest converts travelled from place to place telling the good news about Jesus and the resurrection, there were obviously many questions asked about Jesus.

People wanted to know what he was like. They were eager to hear some of the stories of what he had done and the things he had said.

In response to different questions in different places these stories were told in differing ways, in differing order. As the stories were told again and again, then remembered and told again, they were gradually collected and strung together. From place to place these collections probably varied in their content, their emphasis, and their order. Over time the stories gradually acquired a fixed form.

Told orally and then written down, these collections of stories and sayings were eventually used as the sources for the gospels as we have them today. This explains why we have more than one gospel.

What to Look for in the Gospels

As you read the gospels for growth and enjoyment, I would suggest that you focus on five distinct areas.

Personal Encounters: The stories of personal encounters between Jesus and various individuals are among the most compelling in the gospels. As you read of these encounters try to notice the following:

o   Why do these people come to Jesus? Are they puzzled; are they in need; are they looking for a fight?

o   How does Jesus treat them? Is he gentle or harsh? Does he do what they ask of him? Does he answer their question? Does he raise a question of his own? Why?

o   Pay special attention to one-on-one conversations. Notice what Jesus does: does he steer the conversation to a new topic? Does he plant seeds that will raise questions and encourage deeper thought? Does he agree or disagree with what the other person is saying? Why?

o   In these encounters, what types of response does he elicit? Do the people respond to him gladly? Do they go away happy, or sad, or angry? Why?

Oppositon and Conflict: Throughout his ministry, Jesus experienced opposition and conflict. When reading, take note of the following:

o   Who opposes Jesus?
o   Why?
o   How does Jesus deal with the conflict?

Stories and Parables: The stories that Jesus told have a magnetic appeal. Two thousand years later these apparently simple stories continue to grip the imaginations of sophisticated people. Ask yourself:

o   Why is this story being told in this particular situation?
o   What is the theme or point of the story?
o   How is it received?

Themes: As you read take care to notice:

o   What does Jesus talk about?
o   With whom?
o   Who brings the subject up?
o   What does Jesus say about it?
o   What tone do you imagine he uses?
o   Under what circumstances does the subject arise?
        — is it in a sermon?
        — is it in response to a question?
        — is it in response to some particular event?
        — was it raised in a quarrelsome manner?
o   What response does Jesus get?

Points of Contact with Your Own Life: This is a particularly important area. As you read be on the lookout for points of contact with your own life. Ask yourself:

o   How do I respond to what I am reading?

o   Does this passage speak to some particular circumstance or need in my own life?

o   In what way?

o   Is there some indication in this passage of something that might, in some way, be a good next step for me?

o   Is there some information, some insight, or some new perspective here that could help me or that challenges me in some important area of my life right now?

You will never tire of reading the gospels. The stories of Jesus are as relevant as this morning's newspaper, and they are always fresh. Immerse yourself in these stories. Imagine that you are there in the crowd, listening to Jesus speak. Think what it must have been like to be among the people who had personal conversations with Jesus. Imagine yourself talking with Jesus today. What do you think he would say to you? What would you want to say to him? Try to locate yourself in the stories that you read.

But remember. The gospels are only one part of the New Testament. Be sure to save some time for the Acts of the Apostles and for the epistles. As you become familiar with this material, you will find it every bit as fascinating.

The Acts of the Apostles

The Acts of the Apostles, more commonly known as Acts, comes immediately after the gospels and forms an appropriate link between the gospels and the epistles. This book tells the fascinating story of the birth and early growth of the church.

Acts was written by the same author as the Gospel of Luke. Luke ends his gospel with the story of Jesus' return to heaven forty days after the resurrection, and Acts begins with this same story. A comparison of the first few lines of Acts reveals that both these works were addressed to an individual named Theophilus, whose precise connection to Luke is unknown to us. In telling this story Luke sometimes writes as an eye-witness to the events he is relating. At other times he appears to be dependent on others for his material.

The first few chapters tell the story of the beginnings of the church in Jerusalem. The story starts with the coming of the Holy Spirit on the day of Pentecost. Those who responded to Peter's sermon that day became the first Christians and formed the first church. It is helpful to realize that all of these first Christians were Jews who came to believe that in Jesus God had sent to Israel the long-promised Messiah.

A major event in the life of the early church was the conversion of Saul of Tarsus. Saul was a brilliant Pharisee who had eagerly persecuted the church because he believed that these Christians were dangerous heretics who were corrupting the Jewish faith. The story of his conversion is told in chapter nine.

The remainder of the book of Acts relates the adventures and exploits of Saul as he travelled through the Mediterranean world, telling the good news about Jesus and the resurrection, and starting churches in various cities. Early on in this story, as Saul begins to concentrate his efforts more and more on Gentiles, Luke switches to the Greek form of his name, Paul.

A particularly vexing issue for the early church was the status of Gentile converts in the church. Was it necessary for Gentile converts to observe Jewish laws and customs, or was it sufficient for them simply to put their faith in Jesus? The tension raised by this issue runs throughout the New Testament and features quite prominently in Acts.

This is the issue that ultimately led to Paul's downfall. Returning to Jerusalem from one of his missionary journeys, Paul found himself in trouble. Elements within the Jewish community who had heard of his preaching out in the provinces accused him of defiling their ancestral faith. Riots broke out and Paul was arrested. The story of Paul's imprisonment and subsequent trip to Rome to stand trial before Caesar forms the last major section of this book. The book of Acts ends with Paul under house arrest in Rome awaiting his trial. There is no record of the outcome of the trial, although it is quite certain that Paul was executed in Rome.

The best way to read Acts is simply to sit back and enjoy the story. It is spellbinding. You will want to read it again and again. If your Bible has maps at the back, you might want to check them occasionally as you read of Paul's travels and adventures in various places.

As you read, pay particular attention to what these early preachers said about Jesus: about who he is, what he has done, and why they believed that he was the fulfilment of so much of what is anticipated in the Old Testament. Note the various ways in which they take advantage of opportunities to tell the story of Jesus, and the situations in which these opportunities arise. Reflect on the possibility that there are situations in your life that create opportunities for talking about Jesus. How would you take advantage of these opportunities?

The Epistles

The young Sunday school boy responded enthusiastically to the teacher's question, "Can anyone here tell me what an epistle is?" "That's easy," the boy shouted. "An epistle is the wife of an apostle!" Not quite. Epistles are letters.

Most of the epistles are letters written to young churches after their founding leaders had moved on to start other churches elsewhere. Sometimes the church to whom the letter is written is specifically identified, and sometimes it isn't. (Compare, for example, Philippians 1:1 with I Peter 1:1.) Usually the churches are identified by the city in which they are located. For example, the epistle to the Romans was written to the church in Rome, while the epistle to the Philippians was written to the church in Philippi.

We have letters that bear the name of Paul, of John, and of Peter as authors. There is one with the name of James, one with the name of Jude, and one (the epistle to the Hebrews) that has no signature. The majority of the epistles were written by the apostle Paul to the churches which he or his associates founded on the missionary travels which are narrated in Acts.

Some of Paul's letters were written while he was in jail and are called the Prison Epistles, (see Philippians 1:12–13; II Timothy 4:16; Philemon 1:1–23). Others of Paul's letters were written to his associates in ministry, tò whom he had entrusted the leadership of a particular church, (see I and II Timothy, and Titus). These are called the Pastoral Epistles, and contain instruction on Christian leadership and church oversight, as well as personal words of advice and encouragement to these pastors.

The epistles were written to encourage and enable the young Christians in these fledgling churches to grow in their faith. Obviously these new believers had no New Testament as we do, and they had received only elementary teaching. In these new churches, as young converts explored this new faith, many situations and problems arose which required further insight and direction.

One of the most immediate problems was the relationship between Jews and Gentiles if both were members of the one church. These new churches also had to learn how to deal with conflict and resolve issues of a personal nature within the Christian community. In addition, further teaching was required on the nature of Christian family life and the issue of marriage between believers and non-believers.

There were problems concerning Christian ethics, in contrast to the paganism from which many of the new converts had come. They also needed teaching on the significance of what Jesus had accomplished through his resurrection, and on the distinctive qualities of the Christian life.

Sometimes the young churches faced persecution and needed encouragement (I Peter 4:12). Sometimes bitter controversies and quarrels broke out in the communities and they required a sharp reprimand (I Corinthians 1:10). All of this and more is found in the epistles.

The epistles basically proclaim the significance of the resurrection and call those who believe in Jesus to a new level of living. They explain the content of the Christian faith and show what that faith looks like in action. In these books we learn what it means to live as the people of God — a community formed around belief in the resurrection of Jesus and Jesus' presence in the person of the Holy Spirit.

Reading the Epistles

Different types of literature are read in different ways. Reading a scientific textbook is different from reading a novel; both are different from reading a book of poetry. There is also a difference between reading an epistle and a gospel.

Most people find that they have to read the epistles in much smaller units and at a much slower pace than they do the gospels. Two or three sentences in an epistle can contain enough information or instruction to make your mind swim. Sometimes the writer goes off on a bit of a tangent before returning to the main point. Sometimes it is not entirely clear where one thought ends and the next begins. Some of this is due to cultural differences between the ancient world and our own; some of it is due to the very complex nature of translating ancient texts; some of it is due to the style and personal peculiarities of the author.

With time and experience, as you become more familiar with the epistles, you will sort out a lot of this. Some of it will never be sorted out because you have other things to do with your life than attempt to become a professional New Testament scholar. So just relax and enjoy your reading.

The following suggestions should be helpful to you as you begin to read the epistles.

Read the Whole Letter: When reading any epistle for the first time, read the entire letter fairly quickly. Don't stop to puzzle over words or statements you don't understand. Just read right through it and get a feeling for it as a whole. Enjoy what you do understand and don't worry about the bits that puzzle you.

Read More Slowly: The second time read more slowly. Don't try to read too much at one time. Read in small units and try to isolate one thought or idea that you can reflect on. If there is something you cannot understand, don't worry about it. The next sentence might contain something that will positively inspire you. You might want to make a note of questions that you can ask your priest, pastor, or mentor.

Remember You Are Reading a Letter: Try to imagine the first situation to which this letter was addressed and the first setting in which it was read. Imagine a small group of believers meeting in someone's house. Remember that most of them had only the most elementary of Christian instruction. Think of the excitement with which they had gathered as the word went out that a letter had arrived from Paul!

Ask Questions: As you read, keeping in mind this small group of believers to whom the letter was originally written, ask yourself why Paul might have thought it necessary to say these particular things to these particular people. What type of situation might he be responding to? What is his concern? What is his tone? What is his mood? Ask yourself how these people might have felt as they heard this letter being read for the very first time.

Make Connections: Always try to make connections between what is being said in the epistle and your own particular situation. Is there something in this thought unit that you can immediately connect with your life? Is there some new insight here about God? Is there something here for you to learn, or to avoid, to claim, to strive for, to begin? Is there a challenge here for you to accept, or a new way of thinking about something? Is there something in this passage that will help you to grow?

Additional Tips for Bible Reading

Get Comfortable: Make sure that you are in a comfortable setting, if at all possible. Obviously, the fewer distractions there are, the more profitable your reading will be.

Don't Try to Do Too Much: When beginning to read the Bible, do not attempt to do too much. It is more realistic to set a goal of reading for ten minutes a day, than one hour a day. As with most ventures in life, it is better to start small and think big, than to start big and burn out or lose heart. As you develop the pattern of regular Bible reading, you will know when to increase your time.

Pray First: Before reading take a moment to pray quietly. Ask God, through the Holy Spirit, to help you understand and to give you insight as you read. Pray that these scriptures might indeed be God's word to you. Pray that they will feed you, enlighten you, inspire you, and guide you. Pray that you will be able to discern the areas of your life to which these scriptures will speak today. Ask also that God will touch your will, so that hearing the word you will be willing to act on it.

Get Started: Perhaps the most important suggestion of all is to get started. Don't put it off. There will always be any number of perfectly valid reasons why this is not a good time to start reading.

Begin with the gospel of Mark. Remember to read at a comfortable pace. Decide to read this entire gospel within the next week. Plan in advance when you are going to read, and where you are going to read.

Next, read the epistle to the Philippians. This is a very short book that can be read in one sitting. Then read it again in smaller units on subsequent days.

As you pick up your Bible to begin reading, remember that you are on the edge of an exciting adventure. Be prepared to be amazed. Be prepared as well to be puzzled or confused from time to time. Many questions will occur to you for which you will not find an immediate answer. Do not be discouraged. Amazement, bewilderment, confusion — all are a part of the life of faith. All are necessary for growth. Remember that you are on a journey that lasts a lifetime, and that in taking up the Bible you are opening yourself to the possibility of significant spiritual growth.

Buying a Bible for Personal Use

Attempting to buy a Bible for personal use can be a bewildering experience. Here are some things to keep in mind when considering this important purchase.

Go to a Christian Book Store

Many popular book stores will have a few Bibles for sale, but you will be much better served if you can go to a Christian book store that has a helpful staff and a variety of Bibles in stock that you can look at and compare.

A Readable Translation

Keep in mind that all our English Bibles are translations. (We have mentioned that the Old Testament was written in Hebrew and the New Testament in Greek.) When you go into a Christian book store to buy a Bible you will discover that there are many translations (usually called versions) available.

For many years the standard English translation was the King James version. The name is due to the fact that it was King James of England who authorized this translation of the scriptures. (It is very difficult to appreciate the fact that at one time it was a very contentious issue whether or not the scriptures should be translated into the common language of the people! This translation into the popular tongue had the support and authorization of the king.)

Translated in 1611, the language of this version is indescribably majestic and beautiful. The problem is that it is almost equally impossible for modern people to understand. We simply don't speak this language anymore. Don't buy this version for your personal use! It will only frustrate you.

Recent years have witnessed an explosion of Bible translating activity. There are a number of excellent translations available which combine first-rate biblical scholarship with a clear and lucid style in readable English. Among these are the New International Version, the New Revised Standard Version, and the New Jerusalem Bible. You could ask the consultant in the book store to show you how these versions compare with each other in some of the more popular Bible passages, for example, the twenty-third psalm, the Lord's Prayer, the fourteenth chapter of John's gospel. I would recommend that you make your choice from among these three versions.

The Right Edition

Each of these translations comes in a number of editions. When you have decided which translation you will purchase, the next decision is which edition is right for you. There are a number of factors to consider here.

The Size of the Book: The old family Bible with its hard covers and all the information about the family tree inside the front cover has a certain aesthetic appeal, but it is of limited value for personal reading. You will need a Bible that you can hold comfortably while reading.

The Size of the Type: Most of us are familiar with the pew Bibles in our churches that look as though the main aim of the publisher was to make certain that no one would ever attempt to read them. The type is too small and the lines are too narrowly spaced. Bible reading should be an enjoyable experience, not an endurance contest, or an obstacle course. Make sure that the size of the type and the spacing of the lines is right for you. Eye strain will destroy your resolve very quickly.

Background Information and Reading Aids: Many newer editions of the Bible offer the reader a wide variety of background information and reading aids. These include introductions to each of the individual books which give information on themes, authorship, dates, and the historical and political context in which they were written.

Sometimes they include suggested patterns for daily reading, or more specific forms of Bible study, on certain themes, for example. Three such editions of the New International Version with which I am familiar are: the Student Bible, the Harper Study Bible, and the Serendipity Bible.

Each of these contains more help and guidance than you could possibly imagine. Ask to see these along with any annotated editions of other versions the store has in stock and ask the store personnel to explain the various study aids to you. You will be amazed at what is available to help you in your Bible reading.

Bibles are also published on different qualities of paper and with different types of covers, ranging from the simple paperback to luxurious leathers. These are matters of personal taste and obviously affect the cost of the Bible. Remember that the Bible you purchase will probably be used for many years. A few hours of your time in making a careful selection will pay dividends in your personal Bible reading for a long time to come.

The Real Thing

You have spent a lot of time in this chapter reading about the Bible. Now its time to turn to the real thing. Don't procrastinate. Get started right away.

Questions for Discussion

1. What efforts have you made in the past to read the Bible more systematically and consistently? What was the result?

2. What are some of the ways in which people seek to find fulfilment in their lives? What did Jesus mean when he told the woman that those who drink of the water he offers will never be thirsty?

3. What are some of the lies we believe that lead us astray? How can the Bible help to protect us from these lies?

4. What new insights did you gain from this chapter? What ideas and possibilities came to you as you were reading?

FOOD	EXERCISE
Scripture	Prayer
Community	Ministry
Worship	Stewardship

CHAPTER TWO

Prayer

Learning to Pray

I remember a conversation with a young mother who was discussing her Christian faith. In the course of our discussion I asked her if she prayed. "Oh yes," she replied. "What sorts of things do you pray about?" I asked. After a moment of embarassed silence she said, "Whenever I'm on a plane, just before it takes off, I pray that it won't crash."

There is nothing wrong with such a prayer, as far as it goes. The problem is that it doesn't go very far. Perhaps you know the feeling. There have been times of anxiety or crisis when you have managed to put together a short, desperate prayer. And there have been moments of deep meaning and ecstasy when you found yourself saying thank you in a prayerful sort of way. But on a deep, ongoing basis, prayer has not really featured significantly in your life.

You would like to be able to pray, but aren't exactly sure how to go about it. The good news is that you can learn. The ability to pray is not something you missed out on at birth. When the disciples asked Jesus to teach them to pray, he didn't say, "Impossible, you couldn't learn to pray in a million years." He taught them how!

Throughout life, we learn many skills. We learn to swim and to skate and to ride bicycles. It takes time, it takes practice and it takes patience, but we learn. Prayer is a faith skill. It can be learned.

If you are learning to live as a follower of Jesus and desire to grow towards Christian maturity, prayer will become more and more a regular feature of your life. In this chapter I want to help you start a deeper and more meaningful experience of prayer.

Three Aspects of Prayer

In thinking of prayer, I find it helpful to distinguish between three different aspects of prayer.

Building the Friendship

Prayer is simply conversation with God. Remember that at its most basic level Christianity is about a relationship with God. God wants to be your friend. It is as simple and as complex as that. The death and resurrection of Jesus took place in order that you might be able to enjoy friendship with God.

But the idea of friendship probably doesn't take us far enough. In thinking of your relationship with God, think of a couple, deeply in love, who commit themselves to each other in a lifelong partnership of growth, intimacy, and faithfulness. If their relationship is to grow and develop, the partners are going to have to spend time together deliberately cultivating and nurturing it. They are going to spend a lot of time together simply talking. They will share themselves with one another in conversation. As the relationship grows and trust develops, the conversations will move to deeper and deeper levels.

Such conversations will feature a number of different elements.

Saying Thank You: One of the things we teach our children is to say thank you. This is partly because we want to teach them good manners. At a deeper level it is because we do not want them to grow up taking other people for granted or simply assuming that others exist to meet their needs and grant their wishes.

A relationship in which one of the partners has begun to take the other for granted is a relationship that is losing its vitality and its potential for enjoyment. When a couple stop saying thank you and meaning it, they are heading for boredom, if not serious, serious trouble. This is an easy pattern to fall into. Unfortunately, we all know how easy it is to take God for granted as well.

In the book of Deuteronomy, Moses speaks to the people who are finally about to enter the land that God has promised to them. These people have spent years wandering in the wilderness and now the new beginning is at hand. They are trembling with excitement. As Moses speaks he reminds them of where they have been, of what they have been through, and he talks to them about their hopes and dreams for the future.

But Moses had spent a lot of time with these people and he knew them well. He knew that as soon as they became comfortable they would be tempted to forget about God. In the course of his dealings with them he had developed a deep insight into human nature. Listen, as Moses speaks to the people:

> When you have eaten and are satisfied, praise the Lord your God for the good land he has given you. Be careful that you do not forget the Lord your God, failing to observe his commands, his laws and his decrees that I am giving you this day. Otherwise, when you eat and are satisfied, when you build fine houses and settle down, and when your herds and flocks grow large and your silver and gold is multiplied, then your heart will become proud and you will forget the Lord your God, who brought you out of Egypt, out of the land of slavery. He led you through the vast and dreadful desert, that thirsty and waterless land, with its venomous snakes and scorpions. He gave you manna to eat in the

desert, something your fathers had never known, to humble and test you so that in the end it might go well with you. You may say to yourself, "My power and the strength of my hands have produced this wealth for me." But remember the Lord your God, for it is he who gives you the ability to produce wealth, and so confirms his covenant, which he swore to your forefathers, as it is today. (Deuteronomy 8:10–18)

The simple truth is that God has created a world full of wonder and daily fills our lives with good things. Learning to say thank you on a regular basis is a sure and certain way to develop and strengthen your friendship with God. Begin with the obvious. Thank God for your food when you sit down to eat. Think for a moment what it would be like not to have that food. As you sit in your house, however simple it might be, thank God that you have shelter. Think for a moment what it might be like to be homeless.

As you take time to say thank you for such basic things as food and shelter, you will be amazed at how quickly your awareness of things you are thankful for increases. You will begin to think of your family, of friendships, your work, flowers, trees, birds, beauty all around you, children, laughter, rest, peace. The list is virtually endless.

As you begin to think of everything for which you can honestly and sincerely say thank you, you will be overwhelmed by God's generosity to you. You will also begin to see the world in a different way. Signs of God's presence and activity will appear all around you. They have been there all along; now you are beginning to notice them. You will be pleasantly surprised again and again, and your response will be a spontaneous and delighted thank you. People will ask you why you are smiling, whistling, and humming as you go about your business.

As you learn to delight in God's world and to be more aware of God's presence and gifts all around you, the dark and difficult spots of your life will be seen in a new perspective as well. They won't disappear; they might not even be diminished. But you will know that there is a lot more to your life than these dark spots, and you will know that God hasn't abandoned you. Moreover, you will discover that you are developing an increased sensitivity and concern for those less fortunate than you. Your gratitude will lead to an increased desire to be an agent of God's care to those in need.

A growing, healthy relationship is liberally sprinkled with thank yous as gratitude is genuinely experienced and expressed. You can begin to develop your ability to pray right now by pausing to say thank you to God.

Saying Sorry: Even the strongest relationships have times when it is necessary to say I'm sorry. Sometimes we have to apologize for something we have said or done that has caused anger or pain. At other times it is something we have neglected to say or to do that has caused the damage.

These words are not easy to say, but if they are not spoken when they should be the relationship sustains serious damage. On the other hand, when they are said sincerely they have the power to bring healing and to restore peace.

The better we get to know one another, the better we realize what the issues, words, or actions are that will introduce tension and strain into the relationship. We learn about one another's sensitivities and sore spots. We learn what thoughtful little gestures and words bring joy and delight. We gradually discover what we should avoid at all costs, and what we must never overlook. We learn how to annoy or hurt one another, and we learn how to please.

This is a very important part of growing together. It takes time. A couple cannot know all of these things about one another at their first meeting, or even when they first commit themselves to each other. They are learned throughout the course of a lifetime together.

Saying sorry is known as confession. The General Confession of *The Book of Common Prayer* contains the admission that we have left undone those things which we ought to have done, and we have done those things which we ought not to have done. Behaviours and attitudes that negatively affect our relationship with God are called sins and because we want our relationship to grow strong and healthy, we are quick to say sorry. This is what it means to confess our sins.

Growing as a Christian involves growing in our understanding of who God is and of what God is doing in the world. As knowledge and understanding increase, we become more aware of the things that will strengthen our relationship with God, and of the things that will hurt it.

As we seek to please God we will find that old habits and attitudes are continually getting in the way. We will discover, perhaps to our horror, how selfish and stubborn we can be. Again, the General Confession describes the situation with poetic elegance: "We have erred and strayed from thy ways like lost sheep, we have followed too much the devices and desires of our own hearts." The New Testament puts it as bluntly as we could possibly imagine: "If we claim to be without sin, we deceive ourselves and the truth is not in us. If we confess our sins, he is faithful and just and will forgive us our sins and purify us from all unrighteousness (I John 1:8–9).

The good news is that God knows us well enough to know that in the course of our relationship we are going to have plenty to apologize for. But we are promised that whenever we apologize God will accept the apology and our relationship with God will remain healthy and growing.

As we grow in our ability to pray, we will find that our ability and willingness to say sorry will be an important part of our prayers. And as we do so, we will find ourselves delighting in our growing friendship with God.

Sharing: This is the stuff of everyday conversation. Here the couple simply talk to each other about what is going on in their lives. They relate simple stories of the events of the day or of conversations they have had. There is little in the way of heartstopping or earthshaking drama here. This is just simple conversation in which bonding takes place and the relationship is nourished.

In a growing relationship the conversation will quite naturally move beyond this elementary level of sharing. The couple share their feelings, they share one another's happiness. They talk about their hopes and dreams. They even talk about their relationship, its high points and its problem areas. The conversation grows to embrace every area of their lives.

God loves us and is truly a part of the everyday, routine details of our lives. We can share these with God. When driving to work, or relaxing with a cup of coffee, or going for a walk, it is a good practice simply to share these details in silent conversation with God. You can mention those things that are causing anxiety, or giving you pleasure, or that you are anticipating with excitement.

Simply reflect on your life in the presence of God. You will be surprised at what you are capable of saying and what you discover about yourself, in these casual moments of prayer. In the process you will discover to your pleasure a growing awareness of God's presence in your life and you will sense that your friendship with God is being strengthened.

Saying I Love You: The woman, starved for some sign of affection from her husband, in desperation finally asked, ''Honey, do you love me?'' The somewhat less than romantic husband replied, ''I told you I love you when I married you. If it ever changes, I'll let you know.'' Well that might have been some faint reassurance to the poor woman, but I doubt if it was exactly what she was looking for. Every couple knows the importance and the joy of saying, on a regular and frequent basis, a simple I love you. But like all the other important things in life, this is easy to overlook.

Wise couples build definite times into their lives intentionally to nourish their relationship. These are times when all other distractions are shut out in order that they might be able to focus solely on each other and their relationship. In moments of tender intimacy they take time to delight in one another, reaffirming their love and recommitting themselves to their relationship. Using the language of adoration they affirm each other and marvel at how they have grown together and the love they share. They will take time to say quite specifically what they enjoy and appreciate about each other.

When we take time like this with God we call it praise or adoration. Such times are as important with God as they are in any of our human relationships. They are absolutely indispensable to continued growth.

As Christians, desiring to grow to spiritual maturity and to become everything that God would like us to be, we build intentional times into our lives to say I love you to God and to nurture our growing relationship. We use the language of lovers. We say how much we value our relationship. We express our delight in all that we are discovering about God as we are becoming sensitive to God's presence to us in various ways. As we do so we will find that we are gradually overcome with awe, and we will move quite naturally into deeper and deeper experiences of praise.

Everything we have said about prayer so far is intended to help us to nurture and deepen our relationship with God. We move on now to consider two more aspects of prayer.

Making Requests

I love the cartoon I saw recently of a little boy, dressed in his one-piece pyjamas, teddy bear under his arm, obviously all ready to go to bed for the night. As he is about to leave the room he says to the adults sitting there: "I'm going to say my prayers. Does anybody want anything?"

Making requests of God is certainly a legitimate aspect of prayer. On several occasions Jesus encouraged us to do so. Most of us are familiar with those gentle words in the Sermon on the Mount: "Ask and it will be given to you; seek and you will find; knock and the door will be opened to you" (Matthew 7:7).

In a loving relationship it is entirely in order and natural for the partners to ask each other to do things or to give things to one another. Lovers delight in responding to such requests.

But a relationship is not very healthy if it is characterized almost exclusively by one of the partners making self-centred demands of the other. If this is true in our relationship with God, prayer is reduced to little more than a shopping list that we make out on an as-needed basis and then present to God. This is hardly a prescription for healthy spiritual growth. Unfortunately, this is as far as many people get in their understanding of prayer.

In the New Testament Letter of James there is an interesting little passage that sheds valuable light on this aspect of prayer. Apparently in a rather feisty mood, James scolds the Christians to whom he is writing: "You do not have, because you do not ask God," he says. Then he immediately adds, "You ask, you do not receive, because you ask with wrong motives, that you may spend what you get on your pleasures" (James 4:2,3). James is saying that prayer is not a blank cheque to be used at will in God's supermarket. God is not Santa Claus. Being encouraged to bring our requests to God is not the same as being invited to a free-for-all.

This asking aspect of prayer should be based upon our growing desire to live lives that are pleasing to God. In our journey towards spiritual maturity we are learning to say yes more often and more sincerely to God's vision of what God would like to see happening in the world.

Part of the excitement of faith development and spiritual growth is our increasing understanding of what this vision is and of how we can play a part in it. As this happens, we are more and more able to bring to God requests that are in keeping with this vision and which will bring it closer to becoming a reality. Such prayer is far removed from self-centred shopping lists.

Prayer that is based on such a solid foundation can take many forms. In the New Testament First Letter of Peter we find this beautiful invitation: "Cast all your anxiety on him (God), because he cares for you" (I Peter 5:7). God understands our situation perfectly and knows that we have many legitimate needs and concerns as we go through life. We are invited to bring those concerns to God. We can lay them to rest with God, confident that God cares for us and will never abandon us or forget about us.

There will be times that we will want to ask for guidance or for wisdom in a particular situation. We might find ourselves in a position where we need to ask for continued perseverance in saying yes to God, because we are facing a strong inclination to go another way. We will ask for continued resolve for ourselves and we will come to the stage where we are praying for the growth of others as well. In the Letter to the Philippians, Paul told the members of the church in Philippi that he was constantly praying for them. This is a part of what he prayed:

> This is my prayer, that your love may abound more and more in knowledge and depth of insight, so that you may be able to discern what is best and may be pure and blameless until the day of Christ, filled with the fruit of righteousness that comes through Jesus Christ — to the glory and praise of God. (Philippians 1:9–11)

You will find yourself praying prayers like this for yourself and for your friends.

At times you will be so overwhelmed by the complexities of life that you will hardly know what to pray for. Here too there is good news. Listen to these words of Paul in the Letter to the Romans:

> The Spirit helps us in our weakness; for we do not know how to pray as we ought, but that very Spirit intercedes with sighs too deep for words. And God, who searches the heart,

knows what is the mind of the Spirit, because the Spirit intercedes for the saints according to the will of God. (Romans 8:26,27)

What I think Paul is saying here is that sometimes the most profound and articulate prayer we can possibly offer is a simple and sincere yes to God from the bottom of our heart.

In encouraging us to bring our requests to God in prayer, Jesus appeals to our experience as parents and the desire we have to do what is best for our children. "Is there anyone among you who, if your child asks for a fish, will give a snake instead of a fish? Or if the child asks for an egg, will give a scorpion?"

We temper the requests of our children in order to give them what we know to be best for them. So God does with us. "If you then, who are evil, know how to give good gifts to your children, how much more will the heavenly Father give the Holy Spirit to those who ask him!" (Luke 11:11–13).

Fighting Evil

In the chapter on the Bible, we observed that much of the Bible is simply unintelligible unless we accept the underlying assumption that there are evil powers at work in God's creation, whose sole intention is to frustrate God's purposes and to prevent God's vision for the world from ever becoming a reality.

At its deepest level, prayer is warfare against these evil powers and their sinister designs. This prayer has nothing to do with whether or not the evil powers are ultimately defeated. In the resurrection of Jesus God demonstrated very dramatically that the battle has been won. One New Testament scholar, invoking terminology from the World War II era to explain the nature of our current struggle with evil, said that the resurrection represents D-day and we currently live in the time between D-day and V-day. The decisive battle has been fought and won, but there are still many battles to be fought before the enemy is finally and totally vanquished.

What really happens at this level of prayer obviously must remain an incomprehensible mystery, but it is clear that God invites us to take our place in the battle against evil, and prayer is one of the major parts we play in this war. Such prayer has two aspects.

Protection: In I Peter we read this rather astonishing statement:

> Be self-controlled and alert. Your enemy the devil prowls around like a roaring lion looking for someone to devour. Resist him, standing firm in the faith, because you know that your brothers and sisters throughout the world are undergoing the same kind of sufferings. (I Peter 5:8,9)

This sounds like dangerous territory! And it is. In the gospels we read the story of how Jesus was tempted in the wilderness as he was about to begin his public ministry. (The story is told in Matthew 4; Luke 4; and Mark 1.) This is a fascinating story, and it is certainly a worthwhile exercise to reflect on the nature of each of the temptations in detail. To do so here would be a diversion. We shall be content with the observation that what was being played out here was an attempt to deflect Jesus from his long-term mission with the promise of a more immediate, short-term gain.

As we seek to grow into a deeper friendship with God and to live more faithfully and more consistently the life that God calls us to live, we will meet temptations. These temptations will have many forms and many faces, but the common objective will be to deflect us from our over-all purpose.

Some of the temptations will seem perfectly harmless; in fact, quite reasonable. Who could have quarreled with Jesus had he decided to make bread from the stones in order to satisfy his hunger? After all, he had been fasting for forty days!

In order to deflect us, it is not necessary to tempt us with the classical expressions of evil. Most of us are too clever and too decent to be tricked like that. All that is necessary is to keep us so busy doing respectable and worthwhile things that we have no time to pursue seriously our friendship with God. It will fall away by default. We will hardly even notice. So often, the good is the enemy of the best.

With this in mind, it is worth looking again at Paul's prayer for the Christians in Philippi:

> And this is my prayer: that your love may abound more and more in knowledge and depth of insight, so that you may be able to discern what is best and may be pure and blameless until the day of Christ, filled with the fruit of righteousness that comes through Jesus Christ — to the glory and praise of God. (Philippians 1:9–11)

Listen to these prayers for the Christians in Ephesus:

> I pray also ... that the eyes of your heart may be enlightened in order that you may know the hope to which he has called you, the riches of his glorious inheritance in the saints, and his incomparably great power for us who believe. (Ephesians 1:18,19)

and again,

> I pray that out of his (God's) glorious riches he may strengthen you with power through his Spirit in your inner being, so that Christ may dwell in your hearts through faith. And I pray that you, being rooted and established in love, may have power, together with all the saints, to grasp how wide and long and high and deep is the love of Christ, and to know this love that surpasses knowledge — that you may be filled to the measure of all the fullness of God. (Ephesians 3:16–19)

These are prayers for discernment and perspective, so that these Christians will be able to keep the big picture in mind and not be distracted from their most important goal by more immediate and pressing concerns.

In the passage we read from I Peter, it seems that the suffering they were enduring because of their faith was posing a temptation for some. Perhaps they were becoming weary and frustrated, wondering if the struggle was worth it. Perhaps they were growing disillusioned and beginning to doubt. These are temptations that all of us will face from time to time. Here our prayer will be for perseverance and strength, and for insight that will enable us to be aware of the signs of God's presence to us, even in the face of great difficulties.

Perhaps the greatest temptation that most of us will face on a daily basis will be the simple desire to say yes to ourselves instead of to God. This is a deeply rooted desire that dies very slowly (and in this life, probably never completely). We will contend with it daily, perhaps hourly, perhaps moment by moment. This is the desire that basically prays, "My kingdom come; my will be done."

This should not take us by surprise; nor should it discourage us. It is not a sign that we have given up or failed in our intention to live as followers of Jesus. Instead, we should expect it; we should be on the lookout for it. In fact, our ability to recognize this temptation in its many forms and guises is an indication of our spiritual growth and our increasing awareness and sensitivity to God's presence and activity.

Sometimes the best response to this temptation is a hearty laugh. We should never lose our sense of humour in our spiritual journey. It is especially helpful to learn to laugh at ourselves. When we consider how preposterous it is that we would really want to put our own visions of our personal worlds above what God wants to do in us and through us and for us, it is healthy to be able to laugh at our silliness and presumption. And as we laugh, we can thank God for making us aware of this deep-seated tendency we have, and ask for help in joyfully embracing God's vision instead.

As I write this I am aware of a certain danger involved in encouraging people to say no to themselves. Many people today have been violated and robbed of their dignity and personhood in a variety of ways. An essential part of their recovery consists of learning to accept their dignity and worth as persons and to insist on this from others.

What I am saying here is not intended to contradict this in any way. Being a follower of Jesus never means that we must allow ourselves to be violated by abusers or treated like a doormat. There is no virtue in being used and abused by others. An affront to the dignity of another human being is always an affront to God in whose image we have been created.

The point that I am making is simply that each of us has within ourselves the tendency to want our personal ambitions, rather than God's purposes for creation, to be realized. Followers of Jesus want to learn to say yes consistently to God.

Taking the Offensive: So far we have talked about our response to evil from a basically defensive position. We have talked about being protected. But there is a time to take the offensive against evil as well.

Evil seeks to distort and destroy God's creation so that what is intended to be beautiful and good becomes hideous and grotesque. There are signs of such ugliness all around us.

We are aware of sickness and disease that indiscriminately mar and destroy life. We are aware of what is called natural evil: floods, cyclones, volcanoes, famines, that bring overwhelming sorrow and hardship into so many lives. We are aware of torture, war, and political oppression that carry the naked face of evil and destroy so much of life.

We frequently find ourselves quite overwhelmed by the state of things in this world. We are amazed that a race as intelligent as humanity, with all of its potential for creativity, beauty, and love, could have brought things to such a sorry state.

One day we live in fear that hostile nations, armed with weapons of incomprehensible might and terror, might actually destroy the planet, or at least render it incapable of sustaining life. The next day, hopes for peace rise and everyone breathes more easily. For a moment. But just as we begin to relax and enjoy a sense of hope, we are aware of another terror creeping up behind us. Just when we dared to hope that we might not blow the world apart, we discovered that we are poisoning it.

Such realities are simply too overwhelming for most of us to cope with. We know that they are no part of God's vision for a creation so intricate and beautiful. Paul writes,

> The creation waits with eager longing for the revealing of the children of God;…the creation itself will be set free from its bondage to decay and will obtain the freedom of the glory of the children of God. (Romans 8:19–21)

Overwhelmed and feeling helpless, we turn to God in prayer. We pray for the extension of God's reign throughout the earth. We pray for the coming of the day when evil will be totally eradicated and God's vision will be reality.

But more than that, we pray for strength and wisdom to be active in the fight against evil. We pray for those who are working in the front lines of the battle against oppression and poverty. We pray for those who are working amongst victims of famine and disease. We pray for strength to commit our energy and our resources to this battle against evil. We pray that we will find our legitimate place in the battle and be found faithful in the fight. The battle cannot be fought without prayer!

The Letter to the Ephesians describes the nature of the battle we are called to fight:

> Our struggle is not against enemies of flesh and blood, but against the rulers, against the authorities, against the cosmic powers of this present darkness, against the spiritual forces of evil in the heavenly places. (Ephesians 6:12)

The passage concludes with a commentary on the strategy that the Christian uses:

> Pray in the Spirit on all occasions with all kinds of prayers and requests. With this in mind, be alert and always keep

on praying for all the saints. (Ephesians 6:18)

Because such a large part of this battle involves proclaiming the good news about Jesus in the face of spiritual hostility, Paul goes on to say,

Pray also for me, that whenever I open my mouth, words may be given me so that I will fearlessly make known the mystery of the gospel, for which I am an ambassador in chains. Pray that I may declare it fearlessly, as I should. (Ephesians 6:19–20)

The Lord's Prayer: A Model

When the disciples asked Jesus if he would teach them how to pray he said, "Of course I will. When you pray, pray like this...." The prayer he gave them as a model is, of course, the prayer that many of us have long known as the Lord's Prayer. Matthew and Luke each record slightly different versions of this prayer. (Matthew 6:9–13, and Luke 11:1–4). The differences between the two are insignificant; I have chosen to follow the text of the prayer in Matthew, because it is slightly longer.

Getting Centred

A few years ago, tired of disgracing myself on the golf course, I decided to take drastic measures. So I signed up for a few lessons. When we got to the tee, the teaching pro asked me to take a couple of swings so that he could have a look at my style. Then he started making the necessary adjustments.

The first thing he said was, "Get yourself centred." Then he showed me how to balance my weight and to centre myself over the ball. He told me to focus on the shot I was about to make, to think it over, to concentrate. Only when I was completely focussed and centred was he interested in getting down to the fundamentals of the swing.

In teaching the disciples to pray, Jesus began in much the

same way. What he is essentially saying in the introduction to this model prayer is Get yourself centred. This is how you should pray he told them.

> Our Father in heaven,
> hallowed be your name.

First of all, we remember whom we are talking to. This helps us to get everything into focus. This is God, the creator of all that is. This is God, who dwells in heavenly splendour. Yet God is not distant and remote. God is not impersonal. Jesus says we should call God Father.

(Unfortunately, for many people this image of God as Father is not helpful. Their paternal history has been too painful. This is an absolute tragedy. In our hearts we carry a sense of what an ideal father would be like. It is this that Jesus intends to convey by this image. We are to think of God as the perfection of fatherhood.)

We are being invited into the intimacy of a family with a warm and caring father. But we don't take this relationship for granted. We acknowledge that God's name is hallowed. We don't take it lightly. Basically, we are saying, You are the centre and the foundation of everything; all of life and creation depends upon you. As we enter into the intimacy of prayer we recognize that we are on holy ground.

Your Kingdom Come

Once we are properly centred we are in a position to enter into our prayer. The first request is what puts everything else into focus. We pray,

> Your kingdom come,

and just to make it more explicit we go on to say precisely what this means,

> Your will be done on earth as it is in heaven.

What we are praying for here is the eradication of evil and the total realization and fulfilment of God's purposes for creation. This is the vision to which the whole Bible looks. This is the great hope for all of humanity, and indeed for the entire universe. This is what gives all of life and all of history its meaning. This is the fulfilment of all our longings and all of our strivings.

The New Testament book of Revelation tries to capture something of the magnificence of this vision in poetic imagery which must necessarily be inadequate:

> I saw the holy city, the new Jerusalem, coming down out of heaven from God, prepared as a bride, beautifully dressed for her husband. And I heard a loud voice from the throne saying, "Now the dwelling of God is with mortals, and he will live with them. They will be his people, and God himself will be with them and be their God. He will wipe every tear from their eyes. There will be no more death or mourning or crying or pain, for the old order of things has passed away." (Revelation 21:2–4)

The coming of God's kingdom is the point of all of Jesus' teaching and preaching. This is what we committed ourselves to when we said yes to God and made the decision to live as followers of Jesus. The ultimate in spiritual maturity is expressed in the ability to pray sincerely for the coming of God's kingdom. As we grow, we are being transformed into people who are able to say more and more, "Not my will, but your will be done." The more we learn of God, the more we long to see God's vision become reality.

Daily Bread

Now that we are centred and have the big picture clearly in mind, we can move on to more personal matters. As people who are committed to the coming of God's kingdom, and who are learning to live out that vision and to work for it, what do we ask for?

Quite simply, just for the basics. We ask for our daily bread. For people learning to live out the vision of God's kingdom, luxuries and material gain are quite beside the point. In fact, they can be positively distracting.

Paul wrote of the dangers inherent in pursuing wealth and material gain. His words are worth quoting at some length:

> Godliness with contentment is great gain. For we brought nothing into the world, and we can take nothing out of it. But if we have food and clothing we will be content with that. People who want to get rich fall into temptation and a trap and into many foolish and harmful desires that plunge men into ruin and destruction. For the love of money is a root of all kinds of evil. Some people, eager for money, have wandered from the faith and pierced themselves with many griefs.

After a brief diversion, Paul returns to this theme:

> Command those who are rich in this present world not to be arrogant nor to put their hope in wealth, which is so uncertain, but to put their hope in God, who richly provides us with everything for our enjoyment. Command them to do good, to be rich in good deeds, and to be generous and willing to share. In this way they will lay up a firm foundation for the coming age, so that they may take hold of the life that is truly life. (I Timothy 6:6-10, 17-19)

This desire for material gain and wealth is strongly rooted in the human heart. Jesus himself, in a passage found just a few verses after this teaching on prayer, speaks more directly to this issue:

> Do not store up for yourselves treasures on earth, where moth and rust destroy, and where thieves break in and steal. But store up for yourselves treasures in heaven, where moth and rust do not destroy, and thieves do not break in and steal. For where your treasure is, there your heart will be also.

He goes on immediately to say,

> No one can serve two masters....You cannot serve both God
> and money.

Rather than worrying about how we are doing in the quest
for a higher standard of living and measuring ourselves against
our neighbours, we should remember who we are and what
our lives are about.

> Seek first God's kingdom and his righteousness, and all these
> things will be given to you as well. (Matthew 6:19–21, 24, 33)

As followers of Jesus we are learning to pray simply for daily
bread, as we go about our business of learning to live for God's
kingdom. It is equally important to note, however, that God
does desire for each of us to have the basics. We who pray this
prayer have a responsibility to ensure that all people everywhere do have their daily bread.

Forgive Us Our Sins

At this point in the prayer Matthew uses the word *debts* while
Luke uses *sins*. I have chosen *sins* because its definition is
broader. Here we are dealing with relationships.

This is where we say sorry to God. We acknowledge that
we are encountering difficulty in giving ourselves over completely to embracing God's vision and will for the world and
for our life. To be sure, some of this has to do with ignorance.

Obviously we can't know enough about what God is doing,
or the way that God is doing it, in order to be perfectly in
harmony with it. As we have said, learning more about this
is an important aspect of faith development and spiritual
growth. But this is not the whole story.

We find we have difficulty doing the things we know and
understand quite clearly we should do. And we find we have
difficulty in refraining from doing some of the things we know
and understand quite clearly we should not do. Paul expressed
this dilemma quite passionately in the Letter to the Romans.

> I have trouble understanding myself. I do not understand
> what I do. For what I want to do I do not do, but what I
> hate I do....I have the desire to do what is good, but I can-
> not carry it out. For what I do is not the good I want to
> do; no, the evil I do not want to do — this I keep on doing.
> (Romans 7:15, 18–19)

From inside there comes a deep resistance to embracing God's
vision and will. It's easy to assent to it in general, but when
it comes right down to the specifics of life, it is much more
difficult. So with the vision of God's kingdom in mind, we
confess our sins, confident of God's forgiveness.

The precondition for this is that we are ready and eager to
forgive others, just as God forgives us. So we ask God to help
us not to harbour grudges and resentment. We don't seek
vengeance and retribution. Learning to live as God envisions
the world involves learning to forgive. This is the basis of true
community.

Lead Us Not into Temptation

Obviously, God is not going to tempt us to do evil. The Letter of James states this quite clearly:

> When tempted, no one should say, "God is tempting me."
> For God cannot be tempted by evil, nor does God tempt
> anyone. (James 1:13)

The intention of this petition appears to be quite closely linked
to the one that follows.

Deliver Us from the Evil One

The prayer is that we be helped to resist temptation, rather
than to yield to it. Such a prayer includes requests for protection from the seductive and destructive power of evil, for
strength and transformation when we find ourselves in conflict with God's will and vision, and for insight and enlight-
enment so that we might know what is good and what is

dangerous.

We mentioned earlier that in order to deflect us from pursuing the vision of God's reign it is not necessary to lure us into the many classical expressions of sin. In reality, it is sufficient to keep us preoccupied with lesser endeavours at the expense of this larger vision. Evil is a formidable and wily foe. We need God's strength, God's wisdom, and God's presence if we are not to submit to temptation.

Yours Is the Kingdom

Some of the later New Testament manuscripts include the final ascription, ''For yours is the kingdom, the power and the glory forever. Amen.'' This is a fitting conclusion to the prayer, as it brings to mind again the big picture of God's eternal reign to which we have committed ourselves and for which we are praying. This is the over-arching context within which we live out all the details of our day-to-day lives. Because there are distractions all around us, it is healthy and proper to be reminded of this context on a daily basis.

In this chapter we have looked at three dimensions of prayer: building the relationship, making requests, and fighting evil. Remember, God is delighted with your decision to live as a follower of Jesus, and loves to hear from you. You don't have to pray long, classical, eloquent prayers. Start with a short conversation with God, and take it from there. You will be surprised at how quickly the conversation develops.

Questions for Discussion

1. In this chapter we noted three basic aspects of prayer: building a relationship, asking for things, and fighting evil. How is each of these reflected in your prayers? On which do you need to concentrate in order to broaden and deepen your prayer life?

2. In what aspects of life do you find yourself hoping "my will be done" rather than praying "thy will be done"? What must you change so that you can pray sincerely for God's will to be done in these areas?

3. How is a growing Christian maturity reflected in the way we pray?

4. What are some of the insights you have gained from reading this chapter? What ideas and possibilities came to mind as you were reading?

Community

Cosmic Significance

The idea of the solitary Christian, outside any visible Christian community, is quite simply unbiblical. In fact, the very notion is a contradiction. The miracle that God wants to do in the world goes far beyond bringing a number of isolated individuals into a personal friendship with God. What God wants to do is to build a community of people whose way of life together will be a witness and a sign of God's presence, activity, and purposes in the world.

The development of such Christian communities plays an integral part in God's plan of rescuing the world from the powers of evil. In the New Testament letter to the Ephesians we read that God's ultimate purpose in the fullness of time is "to bring all things in heaven and on earth together under one head, even Christ" (Ephesians 1:10). Whereas life is now often characterized by suspicion, isolation, fractiousness, and hostility on international, national, local, and domestic levels, God's vision is that in the fullness of time there will be harmony, unity, and love.

The Christian community is to be a preview of this. It is to be tangible proof to the evil powers of their defeat and the victory of God in Christ; it is to be a working model of the world as God wants it to be. As we read in the letter to the

Ephesians, "God's intent was that now, through the church, the manifold wisdom of God should be made known to the rulers and authorities in the heavenly realms, according to his eternal purpose which he accomplished in Christ Jesus our Lord" (Ephesians 3:10,11).

In God's wisdom, the local congregation, working to become a community, is a sign that has cosmic significance. No wonder the New Testament letters to the churches place such emphasis on warnings against anything that would inhibit the development of genuine community. Given its high calling, the church simply cannot afford to tolerate such sins as gossip, slander, backbiting, malice, or envy. The only possible code of conduct in such communities is that we learn to love one another!

A Working Model

When the designers of the SkyDome in Toronto called a press conference to announce their plans to build the new stadium, they knew there would be a thousand questions. What will it look like? How big will it be? How will the sliding roof work? How long will it take to open and close? So they had a miniature working model of the proposed stadium on display at the press conference. If one picture is worth a thousand words, a miniature working model is certainly worth many hours of questions and explanations, repeated over and over again. This miniature working model showed clearly the intentions of the designers and builders. It was a glimpse of the future. Here, in microcosm, the future reality could be clearly seen.

In much the same way the church is intended by God to be a working model of the world as God wants it to be. This community is to live as a preview of God's reign. The word *church* means those who have been called out. The church is a community of people who have been called out from the popular values and preoccupations of the society in which they are located, in order to learn and model a new way of living for a world that is alienated from God.

The Salt of the Earth

To those who were interested in learning to follow him and to live the life he taught, Jesus said: "You are the salt of the earth." Salt was an integral part of the life of the people to whom Jesus was speaking. It was salt that kept their perishable food from going bad. It prevented rot from setting in. A community of people who are learning to live as followers of Jesus are called to act as a preservative in their society.

Sometimes it is hard to escape the impression that decay is setting into this society in which we live. There are problems with drugs and alcohol. We hear about (and many of us experience) injustice and oppression, violence and abuse. Many people live quiet lives of pain and desperation, apparently without hope or sense of meaning. Day after day the media bring us new stories of tragedy and horror.

A community of people who are learning to live as followers of Jesus can point to a better way. Their common life can be a powerful and eloquent witness to God's presence and to God's vision for the world. The values they live by, the standards they follow, the causes they champion, the love they share, and the hope they point to as they bear witness to God's truth can have a wholesome and positive influence on the world around them.

Unfortunately, the call to live in a way that has a preservative influence in society has sometimes been misinterpreted by Christians as a call to live in judgment of others, functioning as moral watch dogs. This is an affront to the gospel of Jesus Christ. The Christian community is to gain its influence by modelling a lifestyle of loving, caring gentleness that proves almost irresistible.

Salt also brings out the flavour in food. A community of people who are learning to live as followers of Jesus will find that their very existence enriches the lives of others. There are many people who are living broken, painful, and empty lives. A church community that is learning to follow its calling will be a community whose practical, caring concern is experienced by those in need as a tangible expression of good news.

The Light of the World

Jesus went on to say: "You are the light of the world." This community, through its life and teaching, is to be a witness for God. Proclaiming the gospel in word and in deed, living in such a way as to point to the presence of God, and modelling God's vision for the world, the community is a light shining in the darkness of a despairing and broken world. Jesus put it this way:

> A city on a hill cannot be hidden. Neither do people light a lamp and put it under a bowl. Instead they put it on its stand, and it gives light to everyone in the house. In the same way, let your light shine before others, that they may see your good deeds and praise your Father in heaven. (Matthew 5:14–16)

So attractive is the life of this community that it leads people to praise the God who is at its centre. Seeing this community in action, people come to understand that God is for them. They embrace God's vision for the world and welcome God's presence in their lives.

You Must Be Joking

Sadly, what is being described here as the purpose and calling of the Christian community does not correspond with many people's experience of the church. The sad truth is that many parishes and congregations simply cannot be described as caring communities. Unfortunately, *congregation* is not synonymous with *community*. any more than churchiness w/ Godliness!

If we are to be faithful followers of Jesus we must change this. It is the development of such loving, caring, serving, communities that serves as the evidence that God's redemptive work is taking effect in our lives. Our ability to develop into such a community is the proof that God's transforming power is at work within us.

A major priority for the church, for parishes and congregations, for individual Christians, must be to learn and to be constantly reminded what the church is. One such eloquent reminder is found in I Peter 2:9–10:

> You are a chosen people, a royal priesthood, a holy nation, a people belonging to God, that you may declare the praises of him who called you out of darkness into his wonderful light. Once you were not a people, but now you are the people of God.

A Community of Learners

The thing that has to be stressed about this community is that it is a community of learners. In the parish church where I am located at present we attempt to express this through our Parish Statement of Purpose which describes us as "a community of ordinary people, learning to follow Jesus in our time."

The observation attributed to Groucho Marx, "I would never want to join a club that would accept me as a member," is appropriate to the church community as well. We do not become members of the church community on the basis of a demonstrated ability to live this life. We come into the church because we want to learn to live it. This means that the church will always be imperfect because its membership consists entirely of learners.

This is precisely one of the community's strongest and most appealing qualities. People are learning to love and to accept one another, even though they are at various stages of growth, understanding, and maturity. The fundamental defining characteristic of the community is its love and concern for absolutely every one of its members, no matter how difficult that might be at times. This is a community that places a very high value on acceptance, caring, and forgiveness.

To the surrounding society, the sign of God's presence in such a community is precisely their care and concern for one another, which spills over into genuine care and concern for those outside the community as well. God's reign means that forgiveness and acceptance are in. Suspicion, jealousy, and resentment are out. This is a picture and sign of the future. This is the working model! This is the type of community whose life leads people to embrace God's vision for the world, and to make it their own hope as well.

Many of the instructions to the young churches that we find in the New Testament letters are based on this awesome calling to grow into this kind of community. As you read the Bible you will come across such instructions and exhortations again and again. As you do, try to keep in mind that these instructions are intended to enable these churches to become such a community. It will be helpful here to have a look at a couple of these passages.

In the letter to the Ephesians, following a rather long section that combines prayer with Christian teaching, Paul writes:

> I urge you to live a life worthy of the calling you have received. Be completely humble and gentle; be patient, bearing with one another in love. Make every effort to keep the unity of the Spirit through the bond of peace. (Ephesians 4:1–3)

Reminding them of the new way of life to which they have been called, he goes on:

> Each of you must put off falsehood and speak truthfully to his neighbour, for we are all members of one body.... Get rid of all bitterness, rage and anger, brawling and slander, along with every form of malice. Be kind and compassionate to one another, forgiving each other, just as in Christ God forgave you. (Ephesians 4:25, 31–31)

In the letter to the Colossians, Paul writes in much the same vein:

> You must rid yourselves of all such things as these: anger, rage, malice, slander, and filthy language from your lips. Do not lie to each other, since you have taken off your old self with its practices and have put on the new self, which is being renewed in knowledge in the image of its Creator.... Therefore, as God's chosen people, holy and dearly loved, clothe yourselves with compassion, kindness, humility, gentleness and patience. Bear with each other and forgive whatever grievances you may have against one another. Forgive as the Lord forgave you. And over all these virtues put on love, which binds them all together in perfect unity. Let the peace of Christ rule in your hearts, since as members of one body you were called to peace. (Colossians 3:8–10, 12–15)

Such instructions are clearly intended to help develop, nurture and encourage the type of community God desires the church to become.

Initiation through Baptism

The rite of initiation into this community is baptism in water. Given what we have seen of the purpose of this community, water is a wonderfully appropriate symbol of initiation.

Water Means Death

Water has a dark side that we hear about all too frequently. Water out of control is a horrendous force. Storms accompanied by floods wreak massive destruction and take human life as if it had no value. Water can be an agent of death.

Jesus taught that the way of life is the way of the cross. In the community of people who are learning to follow Jesus, we are learning to die to ourselves in order that we might live for God. We are learning to say no to ourselves in order that we might be able to say yes to God.

In this community we are learning to die to ourselves, because we are learning to believe that this is ultimately the way of life. This is neither an easy process, nor an instantaneous event. It is a direction and a goal. It is often maintained only with great determination in the face of intense struggle. It is a way of life.

With its power to drown, water is an appropriate symbol of initiation into a community of people who are voluntarily learning to die to themselves.

Water Means Life

If the world's water supply were suddenly to be destroyed, life would not be sustained for long on this planet. Water means life. A good water supply can transform a desert into a luxuriant garden.

In this community, as we open our lives to Christ and seek to be faithful followers, we find the water that is the source of our spiritual life. This water refreshes our spirits and quenches our deepest thirst. We, in turn, are able to share this water with other thirsty travellers.

Water Means Cleansing

Sometimes life seems to be filled with compromises and little moral losses, and we may feel as though we are getting soiled and grimy just walking through life. At other times we know that we are guilty of grievous sin, either against God or against a fellow human traveller. Our spirits become weary; we feel like we need a spiritual shower or bath. We can identify with the words in Psalm 51, attributed to King David after he had committed adultery with Bathsheba and had her husband killed.

Have mercy on me, O God,
according to your unfailing love;
according to your great compassion
blot out my transgressions.

Wash away all my iniquity
and cleanse me from my sin. (Psalm 51:1-2)

The Christian community is a place where forgiveness is taught, offered, and experienced. At the very heart and message of this community is the good news that God accepts sinners. "If we confess our sins," we read in I John 1:9, "God is faithful and just and will forgive us our sins and purify us from all unrighteousness."

Water is an amazingly appropriate symbol of initiation into a community that daily experiences, lives, and proclaims the good news of God's forgiveness in Jesus Christ.

From Congregation to Community

Unfortunately, the vision of the church as a community of God's people has suffered much abuse and neglect over the years. For many, the church has come to mean just a building on the corner where people go to hear about God and to say their prayers. In searching for a word to describe their experience of church, for many people *community* would be the last word to come to mind. But community is what we are called to be.

When we compare God's plan and design for the church with the reality which is the experience of many local churches, the question how a local church can develop from a congregation into a community becomes extremely important. To address this question in any detail would go beyond the scope of this book, but there are some basic considerations that are worth mentioning here.

As with most worthwhile endeavours in life, the basic principle here is "Start small; think big." One person cannot realistically hope to transform a parish or congregation into a community, single handedly, overnight. But the realization that we cannot do everything that needs to be done is never a valid excuse for not doing the things we can do. We can make a start, and see what develops.

Building Trust

Trust is the essential ingredient necessary for any community to develop. This is obvious. If people do not trust one another, they are never going to be able to grow into a community. But developing trust is much more difficult than simply saying, We should all trust each other here, so lets start trusting! Such exhortations deserve a place in the dictionary under *futility*.

There are many reasons why trust is difficult to develop. We have been nurtured and formed in a society that values competition. It started in infancy when our parents were convinced that we were making intelligible noises at an earlier age than the infant across the street. It continued with their pride (or despair) when they observed how early (or late) we started walking, in comparison to that same child.

And that was just the beginning! All through school we were taught to be competitive and were evaluated in terms of comparisons with others. In sports this value was reinforced. Even in team sports a "Most Valuable Player" was chosen, and later an "All-Star Team" was selected. By the time we graduated from school we understood intuitively that competition, getting ahead, leaving others behind, is what it's all about.

But if we are always comparing ourselves to others, there is no basis for trust. Such an environment breeds suspicion, which in turn fosters secrecy. The less others know what I am up to, what I am thinking, what I am planning, the better. It almost goes without saying that we are not going to reveal any weakness to them. We will almost unconsciously strive always to present ourselves in the best possible light.

When we bring these attitudes with us into the church, the possibility for any meaningful development of community is destroyed. This is one of the very first lessons we have to learn as we set out to live this new life to which we have been called. We must learn to build trust.

Learning to build trust is a slow process. It cannot be rushed. People are not about to discard years of training and condi

tioning and begin sharing the deepest secrets of their hearts
with virtual strangers. People are not about to embrace a concept of community whose first statement is: Tell us everything
about yourself that you have always hoped no one would ever
find out. They must be convinced that people are really
interested in understanding them and in knowing what it feels
like to be who they are, before they feel free to lower their
guard.

Trust develops in a safe environment where we know that
the others are there to help us and to encourage us. Community flowers when we begin to realize that everyone around
us is committed to understanding us and caring for us. In such
an environment we gradually come to see that we don't always
have to be parading our strengths and accomplishments in order
to be admired and accepted. We begin to discover that there
is actually something freeing about being able to acknowledge
our weaknesses, our struggles, and our concerns in this safe
place.

In the church, building trust has to do with acknowledging
that all of us are learners with a long, long way to go. As we
come to realize that we are travelling together, and that the
best way to make this journey is to help and encourage one
another along the way, community can begin to take root and
grow. If we have to pretend that our lives are perfectly in order
and that we know everything we need to know, then the
development of true community is out of the question.

Most parishes and congregations, even the smallest, are too
large for this type of community to begin to develop on a
congregation-wide basis. It is simply unrealistic to expect people
to begin trusting fifteen or twenty other people, let alone fifty
or one hundred or more! Unless you are the incumbent priest
or the senior pastor of your church, it probably lies beyond
your area of immediate influence to begin to affect your church
congregation in this way.

Form a Small Community

The most important first step that you can take in this area is to get together with a few others (preferably no more than three or four for a start) who share your desire for spiritual growth. Together, you can begin to develop into a microcosm of true community by committing yourselves to an experiment in friendship, faith development, and spiritual growth. There are a number of things you will want to do together in this small group.

Get to Know One Another: Your first task is to get to know one another. This is always exciting. This should be a low risk time. Socialize together, play together, share some meals together. Find out where the others have come from, what they have done, what types of things keep them busy. As you do, you can quite naturally move on to listening in some detail to the story of each other's lives.

Everyone in your group has a story that will never be told again in this same way. Everyone in your group is a unique creation of God, endowed with dignity and spiritual gifts. To get to know one another will be a privilege. As you share the stories of your lives with one another you will have a clear sense that you are standing on holy ground. I have never yet seen it fail. As the members of a group begin to tell their stories, a sense of reverence develops. A human, spiritual bonding takes place. This is where community begins.

Caring and Sharing: As you get to know one another you will gradually become aware of ways in which you can help each other in the normal routine of life. Opportunities to share resources, talents, and interests with one another in complementary ways will quite naturally evolve. You might offer to help one of the members build a new backyard deck; someone might offer to look after a couple's children for the weekend, while that couple take a much-needed break.

Inevitably, from time to time, one or more of the group

will be facing some difficulty or anxiety. There will be sickness, there will be unexpected unemployment, there will be deaths, there will be problems with children, there will be agonizing choices and difficult decisions that have to be made. I have seen groups rally around a member in all of these situations and many more. The support that group members give and receive in times like these is beautiful to see.

I have conducted funeral services for a family member of someone in a group, and have seen the entire group there supporting the family; helping with child care, making funeral arrangements, organizing a reception, delivering meals, holding hands, giving hugs, just listening. I have celebrated Holy Communion in a hospital room for a member of such a group, with the whole group gathered around the bed. I know of business people who have phoned the others in their group, asking if they could meet for breakfast to discuss a difficult decision that has to be made. These groups are clearly moving towards an experience of church as God intends it to be. A group in which the members are making a concerted effort to care for each other, genuinely and practically, is a group in which trust is developing.

Learning and Reflecting: As we learn to understand one another and to care for one another, a trusting environment develops in which learning and reflection can take place. The goal is to develop a deeper understanding of the Christian faith and to consider in what practical ways this deeper understanding will affect our lives.

What we want to avoid at all costs is a situation in which it appears that the group is beginning to function as a classroom for amateur theologians. One man who grew discouraged with his group at this point remarked, "When they open the Bible they never get below the neck." The emphasis must be carefully balanced between learning and reflection.

There are a number of possibilities. There are many short and basic study guides for such groups available from most

Christian book stores. From time to time, someone in your
group might suggest a specific topic or theme that they would
like to investigate. The group might decide to take a few weeks
looking at something to do with a Christian understanding
of money, or with meeting and dealing with certain types of
fear, or with nurturing the faith of their children. The possibilities are absolutely endless. It just requires a little brain-
storming and a little research. Sometimes you might agree on
a Christian book that you will all read, and discuss on a weekly
or bi-weekly basis. If you are really stuck, you might decide
to begin by reading and discussing this book together.

Whatever you choose, the most important thing to remember is to keep it practical. The focus should always be on reflection and sharing how what is being considered can be woven
into your day-to-day life.

As you listen to one another's stories and begin to develop
a sense of what the world looks and feels like to each other,
and as trust develops through genuine expressions of caring
and sharing, you will find that reflection on this level begins
to develop quite naturally. And you will be surprised at how
you learn to help one another in your growth.

Prayer: Over time, the group will also learn to pray together,
for each other. Some people, for various reasons, will always
find this easier, or more difficult, than others. For people who
have never prayed aloud with others, it can certainly be an
intimidating thought. This is another area where the climate
of trust and encouragement is so necessary.

The group that sets out to learn to pray together for each
other must be absolutely confident that everyone there is totally
supportive of everybody else. Even then there will be some
tension and feelings of insecurity. That is only to be expected.
But remember: courage has nothing to do with the absence
of fear; courage has to do with proceeding in the face of fear.

Start with one sentence prayers. If one or two members in
the group are more experienced pray-ers, they should hold

back. Otherwise they will intimidate the others and destroy any possibility of this group learning to pray for each other. Simply say one sentence in prayer for the person on your right; or for the life and growth of your group as a whole; or for help to be able to conquer your feelings of uneasiness over praying with the group.

Some groups find it helpful to take a few minutes for each person to write down a one-sentence prayer that is then read in the presence of the group. If the group becomes larger than four or five it is sometimes helpful to subdivide into smaller units of two or three for people to experience praying with others. Whatever you do, never force a person to pray who does not feel ready or willing to do so. Respect individual sensitivities. The point of the prayer time is to enable the group members to pray for each other, and the concerns that are being raised and shared in the group.

Go at a safe and comfortable pace in this, but remember that your group is about growth. Growth in your ability to pray is possible as well.

Most groups find that they have time to include all of these elements in a two-hour session, including time for refreshments and informal conversation. It is desirable that groups meet on a weekly or bi-weekly basis. For most of the participants, this will quickly become a high priority in their schedule. As you meet and grow together, here are some guidelines to keep in mind.

o Have Fun

Keep things very simple and enjoy yourselves; this should be fun! You are not committing yourself to some form of torture, in the belief that it will ultimately bring you some sort of spiritual benefit. Almost every one of the people I know who have involved themselves in such a group has expressed surprise at how much fun it is, and what an important part of their life it has become. Have fun, is rule number one.

o Don't Give Advice

The second guideline is that you pledge yourselves to resist the temptation to give each other advice. This temptation is sometimes almost irresistible, but your group will be healthier and more enjoyable to the degree that you do resist. The purpose of the group is to encourage and to understand one another, not to be setting out agendas and priorities for one another.

o Respect Confidentiality

The third guideline is to respect the confidentiality of the group. It should be clearly understood and agreed upon from the outset that what is said in the group is not repeated outside the group, ever. These guidelines, in addition to the understanding that you never seek to judge one another, will help to make your little group a safe place where community can blossom and flower.

o Do Not Become a Clique

It is extremely important that your group does not give the appearance of being an exclusive clique within your congregation. The best way to avoid this is to let it be known that the group is open to anyone who wishes to join, so long as they agree to the basic guidelines that each of the present members have accepted.

When you have gathered your friends, and agreed upon these basic guidelines, you are ready for an exciting adventure in community and growth. Let me encourage you to be a catalyst in forming such an expression of community within your circle of influence, wherever you are.

Questions for Discussion

1. What are some of the factors that make it difficult to experience genuine community in our society?

2. The development of loving, caring, serving communities is evidence that God's redemptive and transforming power is at work among us. Why is the development of these communities so important?

3. Why should such communities function as salt and light in the world? What does this mean in practical terms?

4. How do you feel about being a member of the type of small group described in this chapter?

FOOD	EXERCISE
Scripture	Prayer
Community	**Ministry**
Worship	Stewardship

CHAPTER FOUR

Ministry

Doing Real Work

One of the most exciting aspects of learning to live as a follower of Jesus is the realization that we are invited to join with God in doing real work. We long to know that our lives have meaning and significance. We want to do meaningful work. In the Bible we discover that we were created to work with God. True fulfilment in life is to be found in discovering our personal place in God's work and in learning how to do it.

Jesus understood that he was deeply and intimately involved in the work that God was doing in the world: ''My Father is always at his work to this very day, and I, too, am working,'' Jesus said (John 5:17). That was what Jesus' life was about. As followers of Jesus, we too are invited to share in the work of God. Learning to recognize God at work and finding our place in God's work constitutes one of the most important aspects of Christian growth.

In order to find our place in God's work, we must have some sense of what that work is. If we don't know what someone is trying to accomplish it is difficult, confusing, and often frustrating to try to lend a helping hand. Besides, work is always more enjoyable and meaningful when we have a sense of how our personal efforts contribute to the accomplishment of the over-all objective.

Put in perhaps its broadest categories, God is at work reclaiming and rescuing creation from the forces of evil and death so that God's vision and purposes for creation will be realized. God is working now to save creation and rescue humanity. The work of grace, of redemption, of salvation, of re-creation is going on all around us. God is at work in every sphere of human existence.

In the end evil will be banished, death will be defeated, creation will be healed, and God's will will be done. Love will replace hatred and suspicion, life will replace death, light will replace darkness, goodness will replace evil. This outcome is guaranteed, mysteriously yet decisively, through the death and resurrection of Jesus. But there is still work for us to do.

Our part in this work is to live as the people of God. This involves the formation of a community of people who bear witness, in word and deed, to God's truth as revealed in the life and teaching of Jesus and to the victory over evil which has been won through the death and resurrection of Jesus. In a world so often broken by hostility, hatred, and suspicion, the life of this community models love, worship, and service. This community lives as a sign, a witness, a model, and a reminder of God's coming reign.

This work is carried out on two fronts, within the Christian community and in the wider world. In his first letter to the Corinthians Paul says that the Christian community is like a body which is made up of many parts, each with a particular and very important function to perform. In his letter to the Romans Paul again uses this body metaphor in order to point out the responsibility each of us has to carry out our ministry within the Christian community. "Just as each of us has one body with many members, and these members do not all have the same function, so in Christ we who are many form one body, and each member belongs to all the others."

There is work for every Christian to do within the church in order that every member of the community of faith might be nurtured and encouraged to grow towards spiritual maturity. The ministries involved here are many and diverse; they include, but are not limited to such things as teaching, leading in worship, caring, listening, nurturing, encouraging, extending hospitality in various ways, and dealing with matters of administration. The health and effectiveness of the body depends on every part doing its job at the proper time in the proper way. If one or more of the parts ceases to function properly, to that degree the body becomes sick or disabled. As growing Christians we want to find our proper area of ministry within the church so that the community of faith to which we belong might be healthy and effective.

But this community of faith must not become focussed on itself. By its very nature and calling its focus must be on the wider world in which it is set. It is called to live as salt and light in the wider world as a witness to God's truth and purposes. The members of this community are also learning to take their place in the work of God in those places outside the church where they are called to spend their time. They are learning that their homes, their neighbourhoods, and their places of employment are all areas where God is at work and where there are opportunities for ministry in the name of Christ.

Working with God, this community finds itself searching, rescuing, caring, comforting, nurturing, challenging, confronting, and opposing. It takes advantage of every possible opportunity, indeed it seeks to become skilled in creating new opportunities, to proclaim the good news of God in Jesus Christ. In word and in deed it invites people everywhere to move from darkness to light, from death to life, to embrace God's vision for creation, and to welcome God's presence into their lives.

To grasp the length and breadth and height and depth of this work is the goal of a lifetime. Even then, we will only scratch the surface. But spiritual growth involves a growing understanding of the scope of this work, and its various expressions in specific situations. Obviously, the more we know and understand about this work, the more deeply and meaning-fully we can be involved. Deeper understanding contributes to a clearer awareness of where we can help.

This understanding is developed through our Bible read-ing, our prayers, our participation in worship, our involvement in various forms of Christian learning events and activities, and our practice in ministry. All of this takes place within the life of this community known as the people of God — the church.

Christians in whom this learning is taking place are excited, inspired, and highly motivated. A church made up of such people is filled with excitement and power. It is absolutely mag-netic and compelling. It is far removed from a church of pas-sive recipients of religious services.

You and Your Gifts

Most of us feel totally inadequate in the face of such an invi-tation. However, in God's plan there is something significant for every one of us to do. In the New Testament passages that talk about ministry we discover that God has given every one of us a personal gift (or gifts) to be used in ministry. God invites us to help and gives us the tools we will need in order to help. And God gives them as gifts!

There are four passages in the New Testament that speak specifically of gifts for ministry and name some of them. These passages are Romans 12:1–8; I Corinthians 12:1–30; Ephesians 4:1–16; I Peter 4:10–11. It would be rather cumbersome to reproduce each of these passages here, so I suggest that you read each of them.

The gifts cited in these passages range from teaching, to showing mercy, to giving, to administration. There is nothing in any of these passages to indicate that these lists of gifts are to be considered complete. There are probably many gifts that are not specifically mentioned. However, it is valuable to become familiar with the specific gifts cited in these passages, and to give some thought as to which ones God has given to you.

Discovering Our Gifts

God has showered a marvellous array of gifts upon the church in order that we will be able to join in God's work. But how do we discover which gift is ours? This turns out to be more of an art than a science, but there are some indicators that can help us as we look.

What Do You Enjoy?

God calls us to share in the fullness of joy. Think about the things that you really enjoy doing, things that give you a deep sense of peace and satisfaction. Chances are that you are tapping into the gifts that God has given you for ministry, and that within those activities lie opportunities for significant ministry.

What Are You Being Affirmed in?

What are other people telling you you're good at? This is closely related to, but different from the question, What do you do well? Affirmation from others can give us considerable insight into our own gifts since we don't always have an accurate awareness of the nature of our own abilities.

Sometimes we might think we are better at something than we actually are. In those areas in which we consider ourselves to be gifted we should ask ourselves whether or not this perception is being supported by the affirmation of others.

Of course, the other side of the coin is equally true. We may be unnecessarily modest or reticent about admitting having a certain gift which others affirm we possess. This is sometimes due to social decorum; at other times it is due to the fact that the behaviours and attitudes which accompany a particular gift come to us so naturally and so easily that we simply assume that everyone is like this. We fail to recognize it as a personal gift.

When someone asks you to consider some particular ministry within the church, you should assume that they have seen a specific gift in you. You should ask what gifts the ministry or position requires and why you were thought of in this regard.

What Bothers You When It Isn't Done Well?

When we find ourselves disturbed because we see something in the church that is being neglected we should consider the possibility that this is an area in which we are gifted.

For example, if you have a gift of administration you might be very distressed to see something being done in a disorderly fashion, with important details left unattended. Or if you have a gift of mercy you might be the first to notice areas of pastoral care that are being neglected or that present opportunities for better ministry.

However, while this is an extremely helpful consideration in discovering our personal gifts, it can also be problematic. The tendency sometimes, when these areas of weakness and neglect are discovered, is to complain and ask what is going to be done.

The more helpful response is to say, Here is an area for which I might well be gifted. Is there something I could do in a gracious way that would make this situation better? Is there an opportunity for a fulfilling ministry for me here?

Experiment

Another step in ascertaining your gift is experimentation. Try out different things when an opportunity arises. There should be an agreed upon trial period, with a commitment at the end to reflect on the experience and to evaluate it in terms of your possible gift or gifts for that type of ministry. This is where community is particularly important. One aspect of a safe community is a climate in which people are not afraid to experiment and to fail. In fact, failure is to be expected. People who seem to have many gifts for ministry probably discovered them one at a time as they stepped out in ministry, taking risks and experimenting.

Small Groups

Perhaps the very best place for discovering your personal gifts is in the type of small group we considered in the section on community. Here there is an atmosphere of trust in which the participants are able to talk about things that are important to them. In such discussions, clues to giftedness will be discerned. Because the participants are there to help and to encourage one another, they will be on the lookout for indications of various gifts and affirm them whenever and wherever they appear. This atmosphere of trust will also encourage experimentation, because everyone realizes that it is perfectly all right to fail.

Within the normal functioning of such a group there will be numerous opportunities for evidence of personal gifts to emerge. As the group makes its plans, sets its schedule, arranges for meetings, gifts of administration will begin to appear. During the discussion and sharing times, gifts of teaching, leadership, nurturing and caring will most certainly become evident in a most natural way. As community is formed and experienced in this setting, other gifts of caring, mercy, helping, giving, faith, encouragement, will all certainly appear. As the participants become accustomed to discerning and affirming gifts they will be amazed at how gifted this group is and will become excited about affirming one another in ministry.

Clues to Your Calling

We are invited to share in God's work, and finding our place in this work and doing it is the key to the fulfilment in life that all of us long for. One of the most important questions we can ask then is Where is God inviting me to help?

Most of us will never have the experience of God speaking

to us in an audible voice, calling us by name and telling us exactly what we should be doing. Nor will we find personalized messages painted across the sky for us, or have visions when we go to bed at night. For most of us, the clues to our calling will appear in more mundane ways. In thinking of such clues, I find it helpful to work with an acronym on the word *clues.*

C

In this acronym, *C* stands for competence. We ask ourselves the question, What am I good at? Everything else flows from this. This is why it is so absolutely essential for Christians to encourage and affirm one another in the discovery of these gifts.

L

L stands for love. The question we ask ourselves is What do I love? The point of this question is to discover those issues that deeply concern you; the things that you care passionately about; the things that you love. Two people may have the same gift for ministry, and to the same degree, but that does not mean that they should both be using that gift in the same place or in the same way.

For example, two people might have a gift of mercy. They are very concerned about helping those in need. One might be passionately concerned about doing something for elderly widows who are living by themselves and experiencing deep loneliness. The other might have no interest at all in visiting elderly widows, but might have a passionate interest in helping the parents of handicapped children. Each gift can be used effectively and faithfully in an almost infinite variety of situations. The key is to combine your gift with your area of concern. You will be most effective when serving in those areas.

U

U has to do with understanding. Here we are concerned with our understanding in two important areas.

Understanding Yourself: What you know about yourself is an important clue to where you are being invited to share in God's work. The questions here have to do with your personality and temperament.

You might have the gift of hospitality and be keenly concerned about making sure that newcomers to your church are well treated and warmly welcomed. If you are an extroverted person, you might decide that you would like to be greeter on Sunday mornings and be in the front lines of the welcoming process. Another person might have the same gift and share the same concern, but might be introverted. To ask such a person to serve as a greeter would fill him with dread. The introverted personality would probably be much happier helping in the background with the arrangements for the coffee hour after the service, or perhaps helping to set a hospitable atmosphere for a newcomers' evening at the church.

Another consideration is the type of work that you enjoy. Do you like to work with other people or do you prefer to work on your own? Do you prefer to work on specific projects, with a set time limit, or do you like open-ended processes better? Do you like getting involved with something that is already in progress, or do you prefer being involved from the very beginning in launching something new.

All these considerations, and more, will have a significant impact on your effectiveness in and enjoyment of any particular area of ministry. An important part of growing in ministry is growing in your understanding of yourself. This is not self-indulgence.

Understanding What God Is Doing: Our growing understanding of what God is doing in the world and what forms and shapes God's activity takes in the various circumstances of peoples' lives will increase our awareness of the opportunities for sharing in this work and helping to extend God's reign.

E

Returning to our acronym, the letter *E* stands for experience. The question is What has life prepared you to do? What experience do you have? This consideration, combined with a growing awareness of the scope and arena of God's activity in the world, opens up virtually limitless possibilities for meaningful ministry.

For example, you might be a recovering alcoholic or drug addict. Or perhaps you have been through a difficult divorce; maybe you have been terribly abused in some way. These experiences, as horrible as they might have been, have equipped you for ministry in a way that no amount of professional training could ever do. You know first hand what is needed to minister to people in these situations.

I am not saying that God allowed you to go through this experience in order to equip you for ministry. God would never wish that on anyone. What I am saying is that in God's economy, redemption means there never has to be any such thing as wasted time or experience. When we open our lives to God's presence, and offer ourselves for ministry in Jesus' name, everything we have ever done or experienced, good or bad, comes into play.

The examples given above were drawn from the negative side of life. Obviously, the same principle is true of positive experiences. All of our strengths, our professional training, our successes, our joys can likewise be called upon as preparation for ministry. Life has trained everyone of us for ministry in some dimension.

S

Finally, *S* stands for situation. The issue here is Where do I spend my time? Where am I situated? We live our lives in various places, in a variety of relationships, with a variety of responsibilities: work, home, neighbourhood, family, clubs, church, friends, and so on. Within these places, relationships, and responsibilities; given my gifts, my concerns, my understanding of God's work, and my experience, *what opportunities for ministry do I see?* The more we condition ourselves to think in this way, to see the world in this way, the more opportunities will arise.

All of these considerations are important clues in discerning the place where we are being invited to share in God's work. They are like converging lines. Check out the places in your life where some of these lines intersect. Almost certainly, you will find yourself in an area rich with opportunities for significant ministry. For you, this will be holy ground. Here, you will encounter God.

Learning to Use Our Gifts

When we have discovered the gifts that God has given us for ministry, we need to learn how to use them. The basic prescription for learning to use our gifts is the same as it is for the development of any skill: Practice, practice, practice, along with a bit of risk.

The popular muffler commercial contains a grain of wisdom in its slogan, First you get good; then you get fast. This is good advice for people who are followers of Jesus and are learning to use their gifts for ministry. Another way of saying this is equally appropriate: Start small; think big.

One of the most effective ways to develop a particular gift for ministry is to find someone who is modelling what that particular gift looks like in action in a specific situation. Watch carefully, then talk to the person; ask questions, ask if you can join in, and do what you can. Ask for suggestions, ask for help. You'll be surprised at how quickly your confidence and ability develop.

As you become more certain of the area of your giftedness, begin to seek out resources to help develop your gift. There is a great deal of Christian literature available to help you in your Christian growth. A Christian book store can be invaluable here. Seek suggestions from your priest, your pastor, or from Christian friends whose opinions you trust.

As well, many Christian educators and institutions are putting together courses on different aspects of Christian ministry. The best advice, however, is simply to get started, somewhere, anywhere. Remember, the Christian life is about growth. The key to growing in ministry is simply to get started somewhere where we have a reasonable degree of confidence that we have a gift, no matter how undeveloped it might be. The amazing thing is that once we get started and engaged in ministry, other opportunities will begin to appear. So begin with whatever lies closest to hand, and simply let it develop. Soon you will be experiencing the joy of knowing that you are sharing in the work of God.

Questions for Discussion

1. If God's work is to reconcile the whole world, including the human race and all of creation, to God, what do you think might be some of the possible indicators of the divine presence and activity in any given situation?
2. How do you feel about the fact that God has given you specific gifts to equip you for your part in this work of reconciliation? What do you believe your gifts might be? Where do you see opportunities to use them?
3. Do you suspect that you have seen signs of God's presence in the places where you live and work?
4. What new insights have you gained from reading this chapter? What ideas and possibilities came to you as you were reading?

FOOD	EXERCISE
Scripture	Prayer
Community	Ministry
Worship	Stewardship

CHAPTER FIVE

Worship

Why Do We Worship God?

"You Christians," the intelligent young student snorted at me, some years ago on a university campus. "You believe in this God who insists that you worship him. He is so insecure that he makes you tell him how wonderful he is all the time! What an egomaniac! And you actually do it!" She shook her head in derision and disbelief.

She had a good point. Why do Christians gather to worship God? Is worship really about stroking the ego and flattering the vanity of an insecure God? Worse still, does God inflict terrible consequences on those who are foolish or stubborn enough to ignore these demands?

In an article in *Maclean's* magazine a few years ago, Charles Gordon wrote that he had been watching the television evangelists for a few weeks and had finally figured out their religion. His brilliantly incisive caricature of this form of religion went something like this.

The universe is sort of like a three-story house. The ground level floor is where we live. Up in the attic is God; down in the basement, accessed by a trap door is a blazing furnace. We live out our lives on the ground floor. Up in the attic, God spends his days with his ear to the floorboards, listening to what we are saying about him. This, apparently, is all that

God has to occupy his time.

If we say that we believe that God is really up there in the attic, God is extremely pleased with us and causes good things to happen to us. But nothing enrages God more than to hear someone express doubts as to whether or not he is actually there. For those who persist in airing such doubts or, horror of horrors, stating quite flatly that they do not believe there is any God there, the trap door opens, and they find themselves flung into the furnace in the basement. And it serves them right!

This chapter will present a much healthier understanding of worship. First of all we will consider corporate worship, that worship which the church gathers to offer in its principal services, usually on Sunday mornings. Then we will look at personal worship, the worship we offer as individuals in response to our growing awareness of God's presence with us in our daily lives.

Corporate Worship

When we speak of worship, most of us think immediately of groups of Christians gathering in church buildings on Sunday mornings for services of public worship. And rightly so. Corporate, public worship is absolutely intrinsic to healthy, growing Christian faith. But what is happening when Christians gather for public worship? There are at least three important aspects to consider here.

Practicing God's Presence

In this community of people who are learning to follow Jesus, we understand (or at least we are learning) that God is with us at all times, in every aspect of our lives.

The majestic poetry of Psalm 139 sings of this awesome awareness with eloquent simplicity:

Where can I go from your Spirit?
Where can I flee from your presence?

If I go up to the heavens you are there;
If I make my bed in the depths, you are there.
If I rise on the wings of the dawn,
if I settle on the far side of the sea,
even there your hand will guide me,
your right hand will hold me fast. (Psalm 139:7-10)

Because we are becoming aware of this, we are no under illusions as we enter the worship space that this is the only place where God is. The church building has no special claim to God's presence. But we have a problem. In the busy-ness of our everyday lives, we cannot always remember that God is with us. The world has a way of squeezing us into its mould. Try as we might, again and again we find that we have reverted to thinking in secular terms. In other words, in spite of our best intentions we find ourselves living and acting without regard to the fact that God is present in every aspect of our lives.

As growing Christians we want to develop an increasing sensitivity to God's presence with us. We know that we develop skills and get better at things by practicing: an old saying reminds us, practice makes perfect. It would be more truthful to say that practice reinforces, but in this case reinforcement is good enough. We need a way to reinforce our awareness of God's presence in our lives.

So we come, week by week, to enter again, consciously and intentionally, into God's presence. In this space that has been set aside for worship (*consecrated* is the word the church uses) we focus our thoughts, our attention, our lives, on God. This space, where we come to focus on God's presence, is a symbol reminding us of God's constant presence with us in all places. In their book, *Resident Aliens*, William Willimon and Stanley Hauerwas correctly remark that those who come intentionally into God's presence in this way on Sunday are more likely to be able to remember and acknowledge that presence on Wednesday and Thursday as well. So we gather on Sunday mornings to practice coming into God's presence.

Remembering Who We Are

The previous chapters on community and ministry have made it quite clear that living as Christians involves much more than simply going to church. In order to understand worship properly, we must remove the phrase "going to church" from our faith vocabulary and replace it with "being the church." We have heard this so often that perhaps it has become trite, but if we are to grow into mature and spiritually healthy Christian people, we must change the way we think about the church. In the chapter on ministry we said that our work is to be the people of God. This community of people who are learning to live as followers of Jesus is the church. We are the church.

When we understand this concept of the church, we see that what the phrase "going to church" really means is "the church is gathering." All these people who make up the church, these people who are growing in their understanding of what it means to live as followers of Jesus, these people who are learning what it means to be part of a community that is being formed by God, these people who are coming to see that they belong to each other, are gathering together for worship.

Over the years, much public, corporate worship has been robbed of its vitality because of our failure to understand the different concepts of going to church, being the church, and gathering as the church. Many still regard public worship as private worship. They "come to church" in order to say their prayers and "to make their communion." What they are doing, they firmly believe, is solely between themselves and God. They can go through the entire experience without ever having to acknowledge the presence of another person. The only thing that makes this worship public is the fact that there are a number of people in the same place doing the same thing at the same time. But this is just for the sake of efficiency. The participants acknowledge no connection to one another, no responsibility to one another. It is important for us to realize that this is an absolute travesty of what public, corporate worship is intended to be.

To the degree that we understand ourselves to be a community, to the degree that this community is becoming a reality, to this degree and no more the experience of worship will be rich and vibrant. Newcomers to the community will invariably remark, There is something about this place that is full of life. I can't quite put my finger on it, but it is different from other churches I have attended.

All week long the members of this community have been dispersed, living and serving in the world in the name of Jesus. Going about the affairs of daily life, using their gifts, living their faith, raising their families, earning their livings, they have sought to be faithful to their calling. They have been God's people in a thousand different settings, in a thousand different ways. Now they are coming back together. (Perhaps a better name for our services of corporate worship would be *Together Again*.) They come with fresh experiences of victories and defeats, with new stories of faithfulness and failure. Some come flushed with the excitement of knowing that they have lived and worked faithfully this past week. Some come with trembling and shame. They have given in to temptation, they have failed to live consistently and faithfully, they have hurt others, they have acted selfishly and dishonestly, they have sinned deeply. Some come with fears, others are exhausted or discouraged, some come hoping that faith will somehow be renewed or enthusiasm rekindled. The community gathers. It gathers to enter intentionally into the presence of God.

As this community regathers for worship it is strengthened and encouraged. As we come intentionally and corporately into God's presence, we are visibly reminded of who we are, the people of God, and we are re-formed and strengthened into a community in which each of us belongs to the others.

In a world saturated with secular values, the world in which we live and work and play, it is easy to forget that we are part of a great company of people who are seeking to be followers of Jesus. We feel alone. We doubt ourselves and our faith.

We find ourselves asking, Is it for real? Am I deluding myself? Faith seems a long way away from this world I'm living in today.

There is a beautifully poignant story in the Old Testament about Elijah, one of God's prophets in ancient Israel. Elijah had had a difficult day. He was exhausted. He was frightened. He was discouraged. With his physical and emotional resources totally drained, he poured out his heart to God. "I'm the only one left," he said. "Everyone else has forgotten you. They have all gone off to worship other gods. I'm the only one left who is trying to follow you." Elijah wondered whether acknowledging God in such a situation was worth the effort. He felt that he was totally alone. God's answer was tender but to the point. "Elijah," God said, "Sit up and have something to eat. Get some rest. You're not alone. I still have 7,000 people in Israel who have not bent their knees to other gods."

We are not alone, even though it seems like it at times. We are not soldiering on in splendid isolation in our efforts to live as followers of Jesus. We are members of a mighty company. There are millions of us, all over the world, and all around our offices and neighbourhoods. But we need to come out and to recognize each other. As we gather together for worship, we remember that we are part of a community. We see this, and feel it, and we are encouraged. And we are challenged to be there for each other throughout the week as well.

Worship as Witness

We live in a busy world. To those who live outside of Christian faith it is almost incredible that busy people would take a major chunk out of their Sunday morning to go to church. There are so many more productive things that could be done. Time is at a premium. Leisure is important. They scratch their heads and look bemused.

This simple act of the church gathering is worthy of attention. Not many people find themselves in church on Sunday morning simply by accident. Not many are there because they had nothing else to do. They are there as a result of a conscious, deliberate decision that has frequently involved getting a family ready as well.

It is Sunday morning! This is the day of the Resurrection! Jesus is alive! God has come to us in Jesus Christ, calling us from darkness to light, from death to life. Sins are forgiven, death is defeated, life has meaning, God is our friend! Sunday morning is the time to celebrate! This simple act of the community gathering week by week is a powerful, eloquent witness to a world that has lost its way. Busy people lift their heads and wonder. Why are these people taking time this morning to go to church? Could there be something there for me? Could these strange stirrings and longings in my heart that I have never acknowledged to anyone perhaps be met in that community?

In the New Testament we are told always to be ready with an explanation for this hope that we have, when outsiders ask about it. A loving, growing community, truly gathered for worship, calls the world to take note! It becomes a powerful act of witness.

Frequently, this witness begins in our own families, with our children, then with our relatives and our friends. For example, one of our children may occasionally be involved in some sporting activity that calls for a Sunday morning appearance. We explain to the leaders that for our family worship takes priority. Children then understand that for their family this is what is important.

In the Old Testament the parents were told to explain their actions and decisions to their children. It was taken for granted that children would ask why their family was different from other families. What's this all about, they would ask. How come? Parents were instructed to use this opportunity to tell their children about God's activity in their lives. They were to explain how they had been slaves in Egypt, and how God had brought them out to freedom and given them this new land. Similarly, in our families, our decision to choose worship over a myriad of competing claims for our time and attention provides a marvellous opportunity to explain and reinforce who we are and what we are about.

To friends and relatives we can say, We are working hard at getting our priorities straight. We are involved with a group of people who are working hard at learning what life is all about. We are part of a community of people who are learning to follow Jesus, and to be aware of God's presence in our lives. For us, worship is now a priority. We can't afford to miss it. Besides, others are depending on us to be there; it's a community kind of thing. We could then go on to say, Would you care to join us and find out for yourself what this community is all about? Sometimes the offer will be refused, even laughed at. But you will be surprised at how often your words and your witness speak to the very deepest longings of a dry and searching spirit.

Celebration

To the young university student's question, Why Christians would gather to worship God? we answer that there are at least three very good reasons: to practice being in God's presence, to remember that we are part of a community that is being formed by God, and to offer a visible witness to a world that has lost its way. But when we gather to worship for these reasons, what do we do? To this question there can only be one answer. We celebrate!

The keynote of worship is celebration. At times in its long and winding history the church has lost sight of this. In places, the word *celebration* is the last word an observer would use to describe what she saw happening at worship. Formal, staid, joyless, somber; who could blame the legions who have voted with their feet, saying, Not for me.

God is a God who throws parties! Perhaps this is one of the reasons why Jesus told adults to keep their eyes on the children if they wanted to know what God is like. Left on their own, adults develop strange ideas of what worship should be.

God frequently comes across as a crotchety old grandfather suffering from rheumatism and feeling rather cranky. But children seem to know instinctively that God likes celebrations.

We are not mourning at the grave side; we are celebrating the Resurrection. In every generation, the church is called to reform its worship and to recapture this sense of celebration.

Aspects of Celebration

Praise: The key ingredient in celebration is praise. In music and prayer we focus our thoughts on God. As we consider again what God has done in creation, in redemption, in searching us out, in calling us to be a people and inviting us into ministry, we are filled with awe. We are overwhelmed again with wonder, love, and adoration.

In our praise we catch a glimpse, perhaps just at hint, of God's glory, and as we do we are lifted above and beyond the details that fill our lives. We remember again that God is our beginning and our end; we see clearly once more that God is the source and the meaning of our life.

This is not an insecure and anxious God, demanding flattery from weak creatures and threatening disaster if it is not forthcoming. This is a gracious, compassionate God who willingly stoops to meet us where we are, and seeks to lift us to a higher plane and vision. This is a God who comes to us, gently and tenderly, reminding us of who we are, investing us with dignity, giving our lives meaning, helping us to stand tall without false bravado. We want to celebrate this!

Acknowledging the presence of this loving yet inscrutable God among us, we lift our hearts, our minds, and our voices to proclaim from the very depths of our beings our eternal gratitude, love, and praise. God does not need our worship. God is God. The truth is that we need to worship God lest we forget who we are, where we have come from, and where we are going. Because God is merciful, our worship is accepted.

Proclamation: Worship flows quite naturally from praise to proclamation. In worship the Bible is opened, read aloud, and explained. The gathered community listens together as God speaks through the scriptures.

As we listen we hear once more the story of what God has done. The gospel is told and retold — and the matchless story of God's initiative and intervention in our history rings like music in our ears. This is the story of God's incomprehensible, limitless, self-giving love. The community sits in quiet wonder as this story of God's searching and Christ's saving washes over our hearts and minds. We bathe in this story, and as we do faith is kindled and hope returns. We are encouraged and strengthened. We take another step towards wholeness.

Through these ancient scriptures God speaks, inviting us still and again to be the people of God. The scriptures speak to us of God's purposes and God's ways, and they teach us to recognize the signs of God's activity all around us. They teach us how to live; they chastise us for our faithlessness, our fearfulness, our short-sightedness. As we listen, God speaks to us. In response, we recommit ourselves to live as the people of God, and the community is re-formed and strengthened.

This community is formed and directed by scripture. Otherwise, it will surely go astray. The community may assume many attractive forms and take up many worthwhile agendas, but because God's ways are not our ways, and because God's thoughts are higher than our thoughts, it will, without scripture as its central focus, inevitably lose its way, and be much less than the people of God. There are many credible organizations in the world working out many laudable agendas, but there is only one church.

Prayer: The most appropriate and immediate response to the proclamation of God's word is prayer. It is important to remember here that these are the prayers of the community, not simply the prayers of an aggregate. The symbolism is important. We remember that this community lives in and through its relationship with God. In prayer the community gathers in conversation with God.

The prayers are initially for the church and for its faithful response to God's call. We give thanks for the marvellous story we have heard from the scriptures. We give thanks for the opportunities that are all around us to carry on this story. We ask for the strength and desire to live in faithful obedience; we ask that we might show wisdom and discretion in living as God's people. We ask for help to grow in our ability to live this life faithfully, joyfully, and consistently.

Because God's concern is for the whole world and because the work of the church is in the world, we pray also for this world which God loves and for which Christ died. We pray for governments, that they might pursue peace and create a climate for justice. We pray that they will provide a context in which all human beings might be free to respond to God's call, and to grow into the fullness of what God intends them to be. We pray for the downtrodden, the dispossessed, the victims of famine, war, and tyranny. We pray that even in the most wretched haunts of human existence, people might find peace and love and the assurance of God's presence. We pray that the church might be wise, diligent, and generous in creating ways to meet all people in their need.

We pray for the local church community. We pray for those who are hurting, who are grieving, who are searching. We give thanks for those who are rejoicing. We pray for the development of meaningful ministries in and through this community; we pray for those who are seeking to exercise their ministry in various ways, and for those who are looking for their ministry. We pray that this community might shine like a light in its local neighbourhood, and through its common life be a sign of healing and hope, bringing glory to God.

Finally we pray for forgiveness. As individuals and as a community, we need to renew our commitment and to confess that we have missed opportunities or acted from selfish interests. We say that we are sorry. Yet even here the note of celebration sounds because we do not confess our sins fearfully, but boldly, assured that God is more ready to forgive than we are to confess and repent. So together, we confess our sins, confident in God's forgiveness.

Holy Communion: At the very centre of this community gathered for corporate worship is the bread and the wine of Holy Communion. Here the community retells in dramatic and symbolic form the story of Christ's death and resurrection. The original setting of Jesus at supper with the disciples is recalled, and the words and actions of Jesus taking the bread, breaking it, distributing it, and then passing the cup are re-enacted.

What happens here must remain a mystery. The very attempt to analyze and explain it begins to rob this experience of its power. For centuries, the finest minds in the church have debated precisely what this experience represents, and how it functions. Major Christian denominations are divided on the issue. I sometimes teasingly remark to those who object to children participating in Holy Communion on the grounds that children can't understand what is going on, that if a proper understanding of what is happening in Holy Communion is a requirement for participation, the numbers at the altar rails would be greatly reduced.

As the community enters into this experience, the presence of God is almost palpable. As we focus completely upon Christ, gathered up almost beyond time with those who have broken bread and shared wine together like this for close to two thousand years, this recalling of Christ's death and resurrection, the mingling of intimacy and awe, of gentleness and strength, of terror and love, cannot really be described. With outstretched hands we receive the bread, we hold the cup, and we open ourselves again to Christ's saving presence in our lives. And we say, yes.

I don't have to know how food nourishes me in order to be nourished by it. I don't know how God works through this mysterious ritual that was instituted by Christ, but I do know that I am fed by it, and I know that the community is re-formed through it.

I also know that when this community gathers for celebration, as praise is offered, as God's word is proclaimed, as we pray in praise, intercession, commitment and confession, and as we offer and receive the bread and the wine, Christ joins us. Here, on holy ground and in holy time we remember that all ground is holy, that all time is holy. Refreshed, challenged, comforted, inspired, we return to God's world. The community disperses, like salt in the world, to be God's people in a million places, in a million ways.

The words of the dismissal in the Anglican *Book of Alternative Services* say it so clearly:

Go in peace to love and to serve the Lord.

And the community replies:

Thanks be to God.

Personal Worship

One of the central goals of Christian maturity is a developing sensitivity to God's presence with us and an increasing confidence as to how we should respond to that presence. Living in God's presence, working with God, enjoying God's friendship, being part of God's people: this is our spiritual worship. This is faith in action. This is the very essence of worship.

Writing to the Christians in ancient Rome, Paul expressed it this way:

I urge you, in view of God's mercy, to offer your bodies as living sacrifices, holy and pleasing to God — this is your spiritual act of worship.

Paul realized that this would involve a radically new way of looking at life, so he continued:

Do not conform any longer to the pattern of this world, but
be transformed by the renewing of your minds; then you
will be able to test and approve what God's will is — his
good, pleasing and perfect will. (Romans 12:1–2)

Then Paul wrote about the gifts God gives us for ministry. The
logic of the passage is inescapable. As we develop our ability
to read the signs of God's presence and activity in our lives
and all around us; and as we discover the individual gifts that
God has given to us which equip us to share in God's work;
and as we enter into this work and give ourselves over to it,
we find that our lives are being offered to God as a living sac-
rifice.

With the superficial understanding of worship as going to
church, the question is often raised, Why do I have to go to
church in order to worship God. Why can't I worship God
on the golf course, or walking beside a river, or even lying in
bed? The question is not always asked sincerely, but it does
point to an essential truth. If all of life is lived in the presence
of God, then all of life is a cathedral for worship.

The immediate answer to the question is that we should be
able to worship God in all these places. This is the ideal —
to respond genuinely and sincerely to God's presence in every
facet of our lives, no matter where we are, in all that we do.
However, this is a skill that few of us have developed. It is
an attitude that we find difficult to maintain. We have seen
that one important reason for meeting together as the church
is this need we have to remember God's presence with us, and
the opportunity that regularly scheduled services of worship
provide us to practice being in the presence of God.

One of the most important things we can do as growing
Christians is to develop our sensitivity to God's presence in
our lives. It is essential that we become intentional about recog-
nizing the signs of God's presence with us. As with every other
aspect of faith development and spiritual growth, this is a process that lasts a lifetime and that even then is never perfected.

But we can get better at it. As we seek to develop this area of our lives, there are a number of indicators for which we can be alert. Here are four of the most obvious.

Turning Points

It is easier to begin our search for signs of God's presence in our lives by looking back. Sometimes things are much clearer in retrospect than they are in the present. We begin by looking back over our lives in general, and our faith development in particular.

As we go back over the course of our lives we will invariably find that there are moments and events which hindsight reveals to have been significant turning points for us. As we consider these turning points it becomes quite apparent that they were like railway switches in our lives; as we passed over them the future course and direction of our lives was significantly altered.

What is really interesting about these turning points for most of us is how very quiet and ordinary most of them seemed at the time. Perhaps they resulted from a simple, chance encounter, or a casual conversation. Rarely were they accompanied by fireworks. But in retrospect we begin to see how important they were.

I remember so clearly one day sitting in a university library, reading a philosophy text. It was just an ordinary day in the life of a university student. I looked up and saw a young student sitting at the next table, and recognized her as a member of a philosophy class that had begun a week or two earlier. I smiled at her, and she smiled back. I was about to leave for a cup of coffee, so as I passed her table I asked if she would like to join me for a break. Sometime later we were married, and today we have four children.

When I casually asked if she would like a coffee that day, neither of us knew that we were experiencing a major turning point. If either of us had known what a momentous chain of events that simple invitation was setting off, we would have had more on our minds than the normal concerns of how we appeared to each other. We would have been trembling with fear. We wouldn't have been able to deal with it. Probably both of us would have fled in opposite directions. But as it was, we simply drank coffee and exchanged small talk, blissfully unaware of what future would grow from this quiet moment.

The more we learn about God and God's ways, the more we become convinced that these turning points are signs of God's presence, traces of God's footsteps in the pathway of our lives. And if it is true that God works through these casual moments and seemingly ordinary conversations and encounters, can we ever be sure that any moment in our life is simply ordinary?

Locate some of these turning points in your life and think about them. Share them with a Christian friend. Consider the possibility that God was present at these points, actively involved in the circumstances of your life. God works in the quiet and ordinary more often than through the openly spectacular. These moments are easy to miss. More and more we realize that all ground is holy ground, that all time is holy time.

There is a haunting story in the Old Testament that speaks of God's presence. The story is ancient. Jacob was running from his brother Esau. He was going to a far away place to live with his uncle. On the road, sleeping outside, he had a dream in which he saw a ladder that stretched up to heaven, and on the ladder were angels, climbing up and down between earth and heaven. In that dream God spoke to Jacob. When he awoke, trembling with fear and amazement, Jacob said: "Surely God is in this place, and I didn't know it. How awesome this place is. This is the house of God; this is the gate of Heaven!"

As we become aware of God's footprints through these pathways we begin to feel like Jacob. Amazement lays hold of us. Our imagination reels. Could it be, we stammer, that God was in that place, and I didn't know it? Did that quiet conversation, that chance encounter, that difficult decision, really take place at the gate of heaven? Sometimes the only appropriate response is silence and wonder.

Coincidences

When we begin to think about the turning points in our lives, most of us will notice what a significant part coincidence seems to play in some of them. These chance meetings and casual conversations, these unexplained urgings and promptings that led us to do something that we wouldn't ordinarily do; the disruptions from our normal schedules and interests that gradually led us into these encounters and conversations; all of these appear to be fortuitous coincidences. And they might well be. Or is it possible that something else was going on there?

God delights in surprises. God loves to create wonder. I am convinced that God loves to play. Perhaps it is total innocence and purity that gives God a playful nature. God likes fun. I seriously believe that God likes to play various forms of peek-a-boo games with us, tapping us on the shoulder, to see if we will notice; setting things up to cause us to look around, scratch our heads, and wonder.

As you trace back the story of your faith development, the influences in your life, the events that led you to consider belief and commitment, the questions that were raised and the events that raised them, the people who were there to teach, to explain, to model, and to encourage, you will be amazed at how it all came together. It is quite simply true that you are, that everyone of us is, a marvellous story of God's searching, seeking activity.

God has been courting you all your life. Can you locate some of these points in the story of your faith development? Are you aware of strange coincidences? Are you aware of coincidences that are happening in your life at present? Is there a chance that in considering these coincidences you might be able to say with Jacob, God is in this place, and I wasn't aware of it?

The Inner Voice

One of the most fundamental truths in life is that we have been created for friendship with God. It is only logical that God would be trying to make contact with us. Communication is intrinsic to who we are. God is a communicator. Even with the clamour and clutter of life all around us, even with the chaotic busy-ness that characterizes so much of life, we are aware of those special, quiet moments when an inner voice speaks our name. I am not speaking literally here of course, suggesting that we hear something audible. I am referring to a special sense of a presence with us, to inner promptings and urgings, to a sense that an unseen presence is with us, making contact.

Sometimes we sense a word of comfort or peace, sometimes there is a half-formed idea or suggestion, an urging to reach out to someone. We say, Oh, I was going to do that. I just never got around to it. But now we realize that it would have been very meaningful to someone if we had obeyed the urging and done it. We find ourselves being prompted to comfort someone, or to offer help, or to say a word of encouragement. Sometimes we sense that we are being prompted to take a risk that will lead us to a new dimension of personal growth.

It is important to cultivate times of quiet and reflection in our lives, so that we can become sensitive to the inner voice. It is just possible that some of these promptings, these suggestions, these ideas, are indications that you are standing at the gate of heaven.

Unexplained Resources

Frequently, people who have been through grief or crisis remark, I don't where I found the strength. It is a truth of life that the resources to cope so often appear just when they are needed. We amaze ourselves and those around us. I heard a woman remark just the other day, "I think that cancer patients and their families must be given a special grace." I think that woman was speaking more truly than she knew.

God is with us during the darkest periods of our lives. So often God's resources are given quietly in these times, gifts left anonymously at the doorway in the night. Where did this come from? we exclaim. The angels climb up and down the ladder; we sit at the gate of heaven. We live in an awesome place.

All of life is lived at the gate of heaven. Growing Christians are coming to understand that all of life is worship. For this we were created. In this, we find life.

Questions for Discussion

1. How has this chapter challenged or informed your understanding of corporate worship?
2. What is the difference between ''going to church'' and ''being the church''?
3. Where have you experienced worship that could truly be described as a celebration? What was that experience like for you?
4. Where have you experienced some indications of God's presence?

FOOD	EXERCISE
Scripture	Prayer
Community	Ministry
Worship	Stewardship

CHAPTER SIX

Stewardship

What about My Money?

Sooner or later, people who are serious about spiritual growth
have to think about their money. What is the place of money
in the lives of those who wish to live as followers of Jesus? Jesus
talked a great deal about money. People came to hear him
talk about life as God intends it to be lived; they came with
their questions, their burdens, their problems, and Jesus talked
to them. He told stories. He posed questions. He talked about
God, about heaven and hell, about life and death. And he
talked about money. Jesus knew that our attitude towards
money is an important factor in our spiritual growth. Jesus knew
that the place of money in our lives is a spiritual issue far more
than it is an economic issue.

Our culture is driven by money. All of us have been conditioned from our earliest awakenings to be acutely aware of the
importance of money. We spend a lot of time and energy thinking about money. We think about how much we need and
how much we have; how we will get more, how we will keep
what we have, and how we will spend it. All of us deal with
these issues every day of our lives. Thoughts of money are never
far from any of us.

In our culture, the standard of living (defined in economic
terms) is god. It is the ultimate value. The ad agencies and

the marketers are the prophets of this god, teaching us how to worship it properly and with respect. And we love it! The temples to this god occupy the prime real estate in our cities and towns; they have taken the place of the cathedrals of an earlier age.

In the sphere of this god's influence, Jesus' statements about money seem alternately naive and ludicrous. These are not the principles of modern financial planners. Obviously Jesus thought about money differently from the way we have been taught to think about it. As followers of Jesus we are called to develop a radically different way of evaluating the place of money in our lives. How the people of God think about money sets us apart from the world in which we live.

Jesus knew the human heart in all its complexity, and he knew that one's attitude towards money would have a profound influence, for good or for ill, on one's potential for spiritual growth. It was his insight into human nature that led Jesus to counter the conventional wisdom about finances. Here are some of things that Jesus knew about people and their money.

An Issue of Power

Jesus knew that money has seductive power. Almost effortlessly it is able to lure us into its sphere of influence. Before we know it, we are living our lives in its service. It calls us, it drives us, it threatens us, it rewards us.

This is a deep-rooted power. It reaches to the very centre of who we are and what we live for. Jesus ascribed to money almost ultimate power. "No one," he said, "can serve two masters." You can only serve one master faithfully. Somewhere, something has to give. When he said this he was talking about money!

The point he was leading to was this: You cannot serve both God and money! If God and the vision of God's reign is not the ultimate focus of our lives, something else will be. For many of us the something else will be money. Money has a power all of its own. It has the power to take God's place in our lives. Money can lure us into its service.

An Issue of Identity

Jesus knew that left to our own designs, most of us will eventually seek our identity in money and the things it provides. We have been taught to think of ourselves as economic units. Our worth, we know instinctively, lies in our ability to purchase. Our possessions declare our value. We even speak of people's net worth when speaking of what they own.

It is important for us to realize that the drive to acquire is only secondarily fuelled by greed. It is first and foremost a quest for identity and worth. Our possessions tell the world that we are "making it." We are worth something. We have value. We are important. Look at our house, our car, our boat, our clothes. We are getting ahead. We are important people. Our lives have meaning!

Conversely, if we own little or nothing, we have little value. We do not engender respect. We are ignored or brushed aside. We do not matter. How could we? We have so little. We might have many admirable strengths of character, but these are secondary. We are fundamentally evaluated, we find our place in society, by what we possess. John Maxwell wryly comments that we are funny people. We spend money we don't have, on things we don't need, in order to impress people we don't like. "Shop till you drop" is a rather joyless caricature of a society possessed by possessing. "Born to shop" is a tragic slogan of a world that has lost its identity and direction. "The one who dies with the most toys wins" is a haunting cry from the anguished and twisted soul of a society convulsing towards death. Jesus knew where all of this would lead. Because this is so far removed from the truth of who we are, of who we were created to be, it can only lead to heartache.

An Issue of Security

Most of us will inevitably seek to establish our security through our possessions. This seems so natural, such basic common sense, that we would wonder how there could possibly be a problem with it. The problem is basically that the more we rely on our possessions for security, the easier it is to leave God out of our lives.

This is the reason that Moses forewarned the Israelites, as they were about to enter the Promised Land, not to forget about God when they settled down and became prosperous. He knew that they would begin to say, It is our ability that won this prosperity. He knew that they would overlook the fact that it is God who gives the ability to produce wealth.

This is the reason that Jesus said to his disciples, "It is easier for a camel to go through the eye of a needle than it is for a rich person to enter into heaven." It is not that wealth or possessions are inherently bad; it is simply that when our security, or our self-identity, or our reason for living is based on possessions it is impossible to keep God and the hope of God's reign at the centre of our life. An obsession with possessions for whatever reason alienates us from God, from our neighbours, and from ourselves.

The Bible does not say that money and possessions are inherently bad. It does say, however, "The love of money is the root of all evil" (I Timothy 6:10–11). What is important is our attitude towards money and possessions and our awareness of the danger they pose to our ability to embrace the vision of God's reign. Preoccupation with money distorts this vision.

Jesus told a sobering story about a man whom God called a fool. In the Bible, *fool* is a terrible word; it is never used lightly. Jesus told those who would follow him not to call anyone a fool. In the psalms this word is used to describe those who are so arrogant that they claim there is no God or who are so short-sighted that they live as though there is no God. When the Bible uses the word *fool* we sit up and take notice.

This particular man was a wealthy farmer. His crops were so good that his barns could not hold them. We find him in the story strutting around his property, chest puffed out, congratulating himself on his success. He wonders what he will do with all this wealth, and decides that he should tear down his barns and build bigger barns. Then he will sit back and take it easy, enjoying the good life, the fruits of his success.

Then God comes into the story. "You fool," God says to the man. "Tonight you are going to die. What will happen to all your wealth when you're gone?" The man is not condemned for being wealthy. The problem seems to be that his possessions were the basis of his security. They were what his life was about. But there are some things in life that not even money can take care of.

The simple truth is that all of us live most of our lives on very thin ice. None of us is ever more than a footstep, a heartbeat, or a telephone call away from some tragedy that will dramatically alter our lives forever. We have no control over some of the most basic issues in life. We live in a perilous world. Tragedies occur all around us on a daily basis. Even if we stay safe from accidents, we still deal with sickness and ageing. No one is exempt. When the lab report comes back, confirming our worst fears; when a telephone call announces the incomprehensible news that a lifetime of conversation with a dearly loved companion has suddenly ended; beside the hospital bed of a terminally ill child; in these and thousands of other situations, the question of possessions is totally and utterly irrelevant.

Jesus knew that the temptation to place our ultimate hope for security in possessions is almost irresistible. Jesus saw clearly how shortsighted this is. He knew beyond any shadow of doubt that such misplaced trust would let us down just when we needed it most.

An Issue of Satisfaction

Jesus knew that left to our own designs, we would inevitably attempt to find satisfaction and fulfilment through our possessions. But money cannot buy the most important things in life. It can buy only substitutes. Money can buy companionship; it cannot buy friendship or love. It can buy the odd laugh, but it can never buy joy. It can buy amusement and entertainment, but it cannot buy happiness. Sometimes it can even buy solitude, but it cannot buy peace. All of us know that this is true. But it is still so easy to live as though money can bring the things that will satisfy our deepest longings.

How much is enough? is an interesting question. For almost all of us, rich or poor, the answer to this question is, A little bit more than I have right now. We truly believe that a few thousand dollars more per year would make a serious difference in our level of satisfaction and fulfilment.

Yet we know how quickly the thrill of a new purchase or acquisition wears off. Almost before we get home, we are thinking what else we need to complement this new purchase. Another article of clothing would be just what we need; another piece of furniture; another room on the house; a slightly better model of car. It goes on and on.

The truth in all of this is quite simple. Our appetites are absolutely insatiable. There will never be a time when we just sit back and say, I have everything I need, I am perfectly content. The little word that fuels our economy and drives our lives is *more*.

Our true desires cannot be satisfied by possessions. St. Augustine so clearly saw the truth of this centuries ago. Pouring his heart out to God he prayed, ''You have made us for yourself, and our hearts are restless until they find their rest in you.'' One of the most pernicious lies of any age is that the longing in our hearts to know God can be satisfied by the things that money can buy.

Jesus knew all this about us, and more. So Jesus talked about money. He talked about money because he knew that all the things we ask money to do for us are to be found in another direction. He knew that if we are ever to become the people God created us to be, if we are ever know the joy that comes from living out this call to be the people of God, we must learn a new way of thinking about money.

It is not going too far to say that for many of us our attitude towards money and our willingness to learn a new way of thinking about it will be a major (perhaps the major) issue in our growth as faithful Christians. It has been observed that faith frequently has at least as much to do with our bankbooks as it does with our prayer books. We can recite the Christian creeds, and profess our desire to live as followers of Jesus, but so often, our cheque books tell the true story of what we believe and what we live for.

A New Way of Thinking

Stewardship is the word the church most frequently uses when speaking of money. (This word is also used in discussions of our use of time and talents. We have considered these issues at other places in this book. Here, because of the importance of getting our attitude towards money straight, I am speaking only of our stewardship of money.)

Stewardship essentially means looking after what belongs to someone else. Stewards manage resources that do not belong to them. When you put your money in the bank, the bankers act as stewards of your money. They take care of it for you. You entrust it to their good judgment. You express confidence in their ability and integrity. Frequently lawyers, stockbrokers, investment companies, and trust companies act as stewards of our finances.

Great problems arise when these stewards begin to act as though the funds entrusted to them belong to them. The bank teller who begins to use the deposited funds as personal income is quickly removed. The lawyer or stockbroker who draws on entrusted funds for personal use is immediately discredited.

For the people of God, stewardship expresses the realization that everything we have ultimately belongs to God. Followers of Jesus are gradually learning that what they have always referred to as my money is, in fact, God's money. We are managing this money which has been entrusted to us by God, in order to make sure that God's work is done.

Stewardship is not simply a stained-glass, organ-music kind of word with no meaning in the real world. It is far more than just a quaint expression the church has picked up along the way to talk about the money that its members contribute to its upkeep. When applied to personal finances, stewardship is an absolutely radical concept. It goes to the very core of who we are and how we see ourselves. It expresses a totally new way of seeing the world. Stewardship means that we are coming to realize that the money we have has been entrusted to us by God to further God's work in the world.

In the sixteenth chapter of Luke we find an intriguing story, told by Jesus, about a dishonest steward who was mishandling his employer's finances. When his dishonesty was discovered this man immediately entered into a conspiracy with those who were in debt to his employer in order to secure his own future.

Commenting on his actions Jesus said, ''The children of this world are wiser in their own affairs than the children of light.'' The children of this world know that their main business in life is to look after themselves and get ahead. They know that if they don't look after themselves, no one else will.

This is not always the case with the children of light, Jesus says. It is important for the people of God to understand what their objectives are, and to work towards these objectives with wisdom and efficiency. In this regard, we must learn what role money plays in this community of people who are learning to follow Jesus.

Growing Christians are learning that money is a resource to be used in ways that will allow God's purposes to be realized. We are given total freedom in this. There are no set rules or specific suggestions, only the objective. The challenge is to use our imagination and our creativity in thinking out how we will apply our money to this purpose. As we learn more about God and God's reign our awareness of the opportunities to use our money in this way will increase.

Obviously, this perspective isn't developed overnight. The ability to live with this perspective is a mark of advanced Christian maturity. Nor is it something that is settled once and for all. This is an issue that we will confront again and again, probably on a daily basis, as long as we continue to take seriously God's call to live as the people of God.

For most of us, the practical expression of serious, sacrificial, financial stewardship is achieved gradually, with great effort, over a lifetime of learning. Even then, on those occasions when doubts rise and faith wanes, or when conflicts arise in the church, this will almost always be the first casualty.

However, for those who have made this commitment, and are seeking to live the new life that Jesus taught, serious thinking about the part money plays in this decision is absolutely fundamental. For such people here are four principles of stewardship that are worth serious consideration.

Principles of Stewardship

Everything Belongs to God

This is the foundational principle of stewardship. God is not trying to take our money away from us. We are being invited to share in God's redemptive work and to commit our resources to this work. This invitation is always a privilege. It comes from our need for God, not God's need for us. To people who too easily assumed their status as "children of Abraham," John the Baptist said, "God could raise up children of Abraham from these stones."

In the psalms we read the rather obvious truth (although we need to be reminded of it again and again) that "the earth is God's; and so is everything in it.'' In a rather sarcastic passage in Psalm 50, the people of Israel are chided for their belief that for some reason God really needs their sacrifices. Speaking through the psalmist, God says to them, "If I were hungry, would I tell you? The cattle on every hill, the treasures of the earth, all belong to me.''

We Need to Give

It would be difficult to argue with the first principle of stewardship. This second principle might require a little more convincing. The conventional wisdom concerning money is that we have to learn how to hang on to it, not how to give it away. I want to offer three reasons why it is important for growing Christians to learn to give. Indeed, why we need to give.

We Need to Give in Order to Be Free: The seductive power of money is undeniable. But it is disarmingly subtle. It ensnares us without our even being aware of it. It takes us by default. As we seek to find identity, security, and satisfaction in the things that money provides, we are sucked into its power. It wraps its chains around our hearts, our minds, our imaginations. It can suffocate the very life out of our spirits. It can drive us to exhaustion. It can do all these things without our even noticing. This power is so subtle and perverse that we are capable of looking at people in this condition and envying them.

There is only one way. The power of money can only be broken by learning to give it away. The basic question is simply, Will I control my money, or will my money control me?

When we begin to give, the chains begin to break. This can be very uncomfortable; frequently it is painful. Yet once the chains are broken we experience the sheer exhilaration of freedom. Only then do we realize how tightly the chains were wrapped around our heart. Only then can we really understand what Jesus meant when he said, "It is more blessed to give than to receive.'' We were created to give, not to hoard. Jesus wants us to be free.

We Need to Give in Order to Grow: The central issue in
biblical faith is whether or not we are willing and able to trust
God. In the biblical stories, again and again tragedy results
from the human desire to carve out our own forms of security
and meaning, rather than to trust God.

The ability to trust God is precisely what spiritual growth
is all about. Learning to follow Jesus means learning more and
more what it means to trust God and how that trust is expressed
in our lives. But such trust comes with great difficulty. We
find that we are alternately fearful and obstinate.

We have been conditioned through the whole of our lives
to pursue financial security as a primary goal. Faced with this
conditioning, these words of Jesus sound like pious claptrap
if not irresponsible nonsense:

> I tell you, do not worry about your life, what you will eat
> or drink; or about your body, what you will wear. Is not
> life more important than food, and the body more impor-
> tant than clothes? Look at the birds of the air; they do not
> sow or reap or store away in barns, and yet your heavenly
> Father feeds them. Are you not much more valuable than
> they? Who of you by worrying can add a single hour to your
> life? And why do you worry about clothes? See how the lilies
> of the field grow. They do not labour or spin. Yet I tell you
> that not even Solomon in all his splendour was dressed like
> one of these. If that is how God clothes the grass of the field,
> which is here today and tomorrow is thrown into the fire,
> will he not much more clothe you, O you of little faith?
> So do not worry, saying, 'What shall we eat?' or 'What shall
> we drink?' or 'What shall we wear?' For the pagans run after
> all these things, and your heavenly Father knows that you
> need them.

Jesus knew how easily we get caught up in these concerns,
how easily these become the focus of our lives. In their place
he offered a new sense of centre, a new focal point around
which to organize our lives:

Seek first God's kingdom and God's righteousness, he said, and all these things will be given to you as well. (Matthew 6:25–33)

When our lives are properly centred, the peripheral issues will be sorted out as well. The goal of our lives, as followers of Jesus, is to seek God, and God's purposes first of all; and to trust that when we do so, the rest of our lives will fall into place as well. This is Jesus' prescription for peace.

As we listen to this teaching, a million questions, all beginning with Yes, but... flood into our minds. Given our conditioning, this is only natural. But the point of Jesus' teaching is quite clear. Those who would follow him are called to develop a radically new understanding of the place and purpose of money in their lives. Followers of Jesus are learning to put God's vision of the world and God's call on their lives before everything else. It is this understanding that motivates and guides them. Part of pursuing this vision is learning to trust God and not to worry about accumulating money and possessions. Indeed, we are learning to offer our money to God, willingly and joyfully, in order that God's purposes might be realized.

This is a perspective that is developed in the face of great resistance. When we analyze this resistance we discover that the very idea of such dependence on God scares us half to death. The good news here is that God understands this part of our nature perfectly. God knows that we are fearful. At this point something wonderful happens! We are invited to put God to the test!

This is truly remarkable, because normally the Bible warns us against testing God. Yet in this matter of money, we are encouraged to put God to the test. Sensing our fear, God issues this challenge:

Test me in this, and see if I will not throw open the floodgates of heaven and pour out so much blessing that you will not have enough room for it. (Malachi 3:10)

So strongly does this fly in the face of common sense that the only way to evaluate it is to try it. Significant financial stewardship is not a matter of how much money one has. It is a matter of trust. And trust is what the Christian faith is all about. For most of us this will be the issue that determines the limits of our spiritual growth. We must learn to give in order to grow.

We Need to Give in Order to Find Fulfilment: We made the observation earlier that enough is always just a little bit more than I have right now. George Barna points out that most people seriously believe that they need approximately $8,000 to $10,000 more a year in order to live as they would like to. And, no matter how much their income increases, they still believe they need $8,000 to $10,000.

The Old Testament book of the prophet Haggai comments on this remarkable phenomenon:

> This is what the Lord Almighty says: ''Give careful thought to your ways. You have planted much, but have harvested little. You eat, but never have enough. You drink, but never have your fill. You put on clothes, but are not warm. You earn wages, only to put them in a purse with holes in it.''
> (Haggai 1:5,6)

When we try to find satisfaction through our possessions, enough is never enough. Whatever we have is always too little. Satisfaction, happiness, and joy come from meaningful relationships and activities. It is no accident that many people readily admit that the happiest times of their lives were when they had very few material resources. Conversely, many have found that increased financial prosperity did not increase their happiness one bit.

What We Have Is Not as Important as Our Attitude

The third principle of stewardship has to do with attitude. This is a far more important consideration than how much money we happen to have. Stewardship has far more to do with faith than it does with money. How we look at what we have is far more important than how much we have.

One of the biggest lies we tell ourselves is that we will begin to give more generously when we have a little more. This is simply not true. Jesus said that those who are faithful when they have a little will also be faithful when they have a lot. Likewise, those who are not faithful when they have little will not be faithful when they have a lot. The time to learn giving is when we have little. It becomes increasingly difficult as our prosperity increases. Remember those cords around the heart.

In the parable of the talents, the servant who was given the one talent wasn't chastised because he didn't have much. It was his attitude that angered the master. Basically he said, "Everyone else has so much more than I do. It doesn't really matter much what I do with this little bit." So instead of putting his little bit of money to work, he buried it. The attitude that says, There isn't much I can do with the little that I have, is not pleasing to God, who asks, "How can you be trusted with spiritual riches?".

How Much We Give Is Not as Important as How Much We Keep

One day as Jesus sat in the temple with his disciples, people came by with their offerings for the temple. Some of the people were quite rich, and they made sizeable donations. Among them was a poor widow who dropped in her gift of only a few pennies. Perhaps someone laughed, or remarked how little help such a small offering would be. At any rate, Jesus pointed out to his disciples that this widow had actually given more than all the others.

Seeing their surprise at this remark, he explained that all the others had given from their wealth. They still had lots left. But this woman had given from her poverty. She had nothing left. In the eyes of God, her gift amounted to more than theirs. We have learned to be surprised by God. God evaluates things differently from the way we do. In this matter of financial stewardship it is important for growing Christians to remember that how much we hold back is far more important than how much we give. Once again the issue comes back to whether or not we will allow Jesus to free us from the power of money, and to what degree we will able to grow to trust God.

How Much Should I Give?

When these four biblical principles of stewardship have been considered, we are left with the very practical question of How much should I give? There are several things to consider here.

First of all, the question should never be How much do I have to give? or, worse still, How little can I get away with giving? Nor is the question How much does the church need? or What is my fair share? The most important question any of us can ask in this matter is simply, How much do I *need* to give? How much do I need to give in order to break money's power over me? How much do I need to give in order to grow significantly in my ability to trust God? How much do I need to give in order to begin changing my perspective about the place and purpose of money in my life?

Give until You Feel Stretched

When you begin to give generously, as one seeking to grow as a follower of Jesus, you should begin at a level at which you feel challenged. As you contemplate writing the cheque or making the offering, it should be of such an amount that you momentarily think I can't really afford to do this. At that point, you know that you are being stretched. You will feel some hesitation, some discomfort, some fear. This means that the chains around your heart are stretching. They are about to be broken. Freedom is not far away. Go ahead! Test God!

Give until It Feels Good

Frequently we are exhorted by some cause or other ''to give

until it hurts." I strongly disagree with this. It is one thing
to be stretched and challenged. But if giving really hurts us,
then we still haven't got the picture. What we want to do is
to break through the discomfort zone until we are free. We
want to give until it starts to feel good. We want to give until
it becomes intoxicating. Remember that we were made to be
givers, but we have been socialized by a world that has lost
its direction into believing that we are supposed to be keepers.

Paul spoke quite directly to this question of how much we
should give. "Each one of you must give as you have made
up your mind, not reluctantly or under compulsion, for God
loves a cheerful giver" (II Corinthians 9:7).

Start Now

This is an area in which it is notoriously easy to procrastinate.
There will always be a plentiful supply of valid reasons why
now is not the right time to begin developing a healthy pattern of giving. It is so easy to convince ourselves that in just
a few months, or at this time next year, we will be in a better
position. We have an incredible capacity to convince ourselves
of things that have little relation to reality.

Nor is it a good idea to wait until we begin to experience
some sort of character transformation in this area. We will never
make progress here if we just close our eyes, clench our fists,
and hope for our perspective to be miraculously altered. The
truth is that the transformation of perspective occurs as we begin
to practice giving. It's a lot like swimming. We can read about
it; we can think about it; we can watch others do it. But we
really begin to learn how to swim when we get into the pool
and start. The time to start with serious financial stewardship
is now.

Getting serious about stewardship is like a young child taking the first dive, or the first roller coaster ride, or the first
trip down the ski slope. Before you begin you feel terrified
or, at the very least, reluctant. But before long you are totally

caught up in the sheer exhilarating joy of the adventure. As in every other area of life, the invitation of Jesus is an invitation to excitement and adventure.

There are several places in the Bible that talk about tithing. Tithing, literally, means giving ten per cent. A true tither is one who gives ten per cent of his or her income to the work of God's kingdom. I am not personally convinced that the biblical standard for Christian believers is ten per cent. Some will find such a level of giving absolutely impossible to maintain in their circumstances. For others, ten per cent will hardly amount to a challenge.

Nevertheless, we do need some bench-mark to guide us in our giving, and a tithe seems a reasonable goal to begin with. My suggestion for beginners is that you set a goal of moving towards becoming a tither, and develop a definite plan for getting there. It is important to be deliberate about this, and to move at a comfortable pace, as you begin to experience how it feels, and as you learn to trust God, one step at a time. But remember that there is a great difference between being slowly deliberate and intentional, and dragging your feet.

Many people have found it helpful to start by determining what they gave last year, and increasing that by a total of one per cent of their household income. This is a significant step, but one which all of us can achieve, except in very exceptional circumstances. Begin here, and continue to increase your giving by one per cent of your income each year. As you do, you will sense that you are being stretched, and that you are growing spiritually. You will find that you are being changed, and you will feel as if you are making real progress. You will feel good about yourself.

Remember that discipleship is a process, not an event. It is a direction for life. As you continue to pay attention to this part of your Christian growth, keep in mind these words of Paul:

You know the grace of our Lord Jesus Christ, that though he was rich, yet for your sakes he became poor, so that you through his poverty might become rich. (II Corinthians 8:9)

In the final analysis, stewardship is the overflow of a grateful heart, in response to all that Jesus has done for us. Such gratitude never asks, How much must I give? The only question worth asking is How much can I give?

Questions for Discussion

1. Why is the question of how we think about our money so important for our potential for spiritual growth?
2. How do you feel about the word *stewardship* with its implication that you are looking after money that has been entrusted to you by God for God's work?
3. Think and talk about the idea that the central issue in good stewardship is not what your church needs you to give, but rather how much you need give in order to be free to grow?
4. What insights have you gained from reading this chapter? What ideas and possibilities came to mind as you were reading?

Where Do I Go From Here?

In the Introduction we said that careful, balanced attention to the elements listed in the Grid for Growth will result in healthy, balanced spiritual growth. Now that we have had the opportunity to consider each of these elements on its own, the question is What next? In other words, Where should you go from here in living out your decision to be an intentional follower of Jesus?

The biblical word for one who is learning to follow Jesus is *disciple*. As one who has made this decision for your life, you are a genuine disciple of Jesus. That might strike you as a rather formal and sophisticated description for everyday people like you or me, but disciples are what we are. Disciple simply means learner. A disciple of Jesus is one who is following Jesus in order to learn from him.

The following acrostic on the word disciple might be of help to you in thinking about your next steps on this journey with Jesus.

D stands for dream. Dream a little bit about the type of person you would like to be. Develop a vision of the person God is calling you to be. Imagine yourself to be that person in the making. Have a sense of what you might be like when God has had a chance to do significant work in your life over a long period of time. Look in the mirror and try to see yourself as that person.

I stands for inventory. Take inventory of where you are now in terms of your Christian development. What are your strengths; what are your weaknesses? What are you most in need of at this moment for your continued growth? Do you need more information; do you need to work on some skill or habit; do you need some opportunity for practical ministry? Give this serious thought. What is the next thing you need the most? Think about how you can get it.

S stands for start. This is the time to get started. Don't delay. There will always be a thousand legitimate reasons why this is not the right time for you. But those reasons will always be there. There is only one time to get started and that time is now.

C stands for cost. Count the cost of following Jesus. Read the ninth chapter of Luke's gospel, verses 57-62. There you will find some very clear indications of what it will cost to live as a follower of Jesus. The incidents recorded there indicate that to follow Jesus will inevitably cause discomfort, disruption, and displacement. Following Jesus is not a diversion along the way, but rather a direction for the whole of life. There is a cost. But there is also a cost involved in not following Jesus; especially once you have heard his invitation to you. There is the cost of dissatisfaction, of lost opportunity, of being unhappy with yourself and the life you are living. There is the haunting fear or regret of knowingly settling for the second best in life; of missing out on what is truly worthwhile and fulfilling. There is the tragedy of not embracing the Truth. Count the cost; and step out.

I stands for inform. Tell a friend about your decision and determination to live intentionally as a follower of Jesus. Share this with someone you trust, someone whose opinion matters to you, someone who will encourage you to give it all you've got. It is sometimes so difficult for us to talk with others about the things that matter the most to us. You will be surprised at how helpful it will be for you to share this simply with someone who will respect what it means for you.

Involve others in your growth and development because you

cannot make it on your own. Join with a group of similarly minded and intentioned people who meet together regularly for encouragement and support. You might have to put a lot of energy into finding or beginning such a group. Whatever it takes will be worth it. We are talking here about the very fundamental issues of life. This is your life. It is the only one you have. You will need a group. Find one or form one.

P stands for patience. Disciples must be patient. Character transformation and spiritual growth are a process, not an event. It does not happen overnight; it happens over a lifetime. You have embarked on a lifelong journey. The art is to embrace the long view, while not forgetting the importance of the present moment. These must be held in balance.

L stands for laugh. You will have to learn to laugh at yourself. What you are undertaking seems, on the surface, absolutely preposterous. Imagine: you, a follower of Jesus! Imagine: you, becoming like Jesus! Imagine: you, sharing in God's work! Laugh about it. Laugh because it sounds so ridiculous. Laugh with sheer delight because it is true. By God's grace, it is true!

You will make a lot of mistakes; even some very foolish ones. At times you will be discouraged or even disgusted with yourself. So learn to laugh at yourself. This will prove invaluable. Remember, the completion of this work depends on God. As Paul wrote in the letter to the Philippians, "I am confident that God, who began a good work in you, will carry it on to completion until the day of Christ Jesus" (Philippians 1:6). Growing Christians laugh at themselves, but they take God very seriously.

E stands for expect. Expect great things to happen in you and through you; not necessarily spectacular things, but great things. Remember, it is God who has called you, and God is faithful. In a marvellous passage in the letter to the Ephesians, Paul writes,

Now to God who is able to do immeasurably more than all

we ask or imagine, according to his power that is at work within us, to God be glory in the church and in Christ Jesus throughout all generations, for ever and ever! Amen. (Ephesians 3:20–21)

God wants to do more in you and through you than you have ever imagined. Glory to God in the church, and in Christ Jesus, and in you!

Jesus is inviting you on the adventure of a lifetime. Go for it!